INNOVATIVE
TECHNIQUES FOR
LARGE-GROUP
INSTRUCTION

INNOVATIVE
TECHNIQUES FOR
LARGE-GROUP
INSTRUCTION

An NSTA Press
Journals Collection

NATIONAL SCIENCE TEACHERS ASSOCIATION

Arlington, Virginia

Claire Reinburg, Director
Judy Cusick, Associate Editor
Carol Duval, Associate Editor
Betty Smith, Associate Editor
Linda Olliver, Cover Design

ART AND DESIGN Linda Olliver, Director
NSTA WEB Tim Weber, Webmaster
PERIODICALS PUBLISHING Shelley Carey, Director
PRINTING AND PRODUCTION Catherine Lorrain-Hale, Director
    Nguyet Tran, Assistant Production Manager
    Jack Parker, Desktop Publishing Specialist
PUBLICATIONS OPERATIONS Erin Miller, Manager
sciLINKS Tyson Brown, Manager

NATIONAL SCIENCE TEACHERS ASSOCIATION
Gerald F. Wheeler, Executive Director
David Beacom, Publisher

Featuring sciLINKS®—a new way of connecting text and the Internet. Up-to-the-minute online content, classroom ideas, and other materials are just a click away. Go to page x to learn more about this new educational resource.

Innovative Techniques for Large-Group Instruction
NSTA Stock Number: PB168X
ISBN: 0-87355-204-0
Library of Congress Control Number: 2002101367
Printed in the USA by IPC Communication Services
Printed on recycled paper
02   5 4 3 2 1

NSTA PRESS
1840 Wilson Boulevard
Arlington, Virginia 22201-3000
www.nsta.org

CONTENTS

MODERN INFORMATION TECHNOLOGY

ACTION RESEARCH AND ASSESSMENT

Acknowledgments

The fourteen articles in *Innovative Techniques for Large-Group Instruction* were selected from the *Journal of College Science Teaching* (1997–2002) by a committee of higher education science faculty. The committee was headed by Timothy M. Cooney, professor of Earth science and science education at the University of Northern Iowa and chairperson and director of the National Science Teachers Association's (NSTA) Committee on College Science Teaching. Also on the selection committee were Daniel Brovey, director and professor of science and technology education, Queens College; Rita Hoots, professor at Woodland Community College; and Gerald Summers, associate professor of biological sciences at the University of Missouri.

At NSTA, Claudia Link, managing editor of the *Journal of College Science Teaching*, made the initial contacts for the book, Judy Cusick acted as the project editor, Linda Olliver designed the cover, and Catherine Lorrain-Hale coordinated book layout, production, and printing.

Introduction

Large college science classes, taught via the lecture method, still predominate across college campuses in the United States. Administrators often favor these large, and mostly introductory, science classes because they appear to be financially efficient and generate large numbers of student credit hours. A department with a limited number of faculty can handle many more students by having classes held in large lecture halls or auditoriums. *Innovative Techniques for Large-Group Instruction* presents effective ways to stimulate active learning in classes with more than fifty students. Reviewers for this collection selected articles from the *Journal of College Science Teaching* that tell us what research says about effective large-group instruction and that show us how college science faculty have successfully modified their lecture courses to stimulate active learning.

An assessment of popular teaching styles and their effectiveness are presented by Leonard in his article, "How Do College Students Best Learn Science?" Leonard first presents research evidence that the dominant lecture method just does not seem to work as an effective tool for teaching. Then he discusses the effectiveness of constructivist learning, followed by evidence that college students have various learning styles that college science faculty should take into consideration when preparing to teach. Leonard's article concludes with recommendations that provide sound and proven ideas for enhancing learning in college science.

In "Are We Cultivating 'Couch Potatoes' in Our College Science Lectures?" Lord tells about an invitation to sit in on a colleague's large biology class at another university. He describes what he observed and how he was unable to admit to his colleague that the students didn't pay much attention during the lecture and that they probably didn't learn a great deal. The drive back to his own university provided time for Lord to reflect on the lecture method and the reluctance of science professors to give up that method.

The remaining articles in this compendium describe how college science professors instituted active learning in their large classes. Many of these strategies align well with Leonard's recommendations. Some techniques incorporate the use of current information technology. We learn also, in many cases, how and why these professors gave up the "lecture only" method. For example, Caprio and Micikas describe how to make the transition from traditional teaching practices to those that are student centered in their article "Getting There from Here." They discuss two forms of barriers to this transition and present arguments against these barriers. The article concludes with suggestions on how to use the many resources available to faculty members who want to move their classes away from the standard lecture format to a more active learning environment.

Klionsky presents a quiz-based, group-learning approach that he adapted for very large sections of introductory biology. In "Constructing Knowledge in the Lecture Hall," he describes a format for teaching that encourages student preparation prior to class and uses problem solving instead of excessive lecturing. Klionsky follows his description with discussions about the concerns and benefits of this approach.

As presented in "Active Learning in the Lecture Hall," Anderson tells how she modified course requirements and engaged students in a variety of active learning activities. In her nonlaboratory Problems of the Environment course for nonscience majors, she used essays, special team presentations, a garden project, drawings, and concept mapping to challenge students to apply their knowledge in meaningful ways. Although she describes these techniques as successful, Anderson cautions that designing a course to elicit active learning takes time to design and is challenging for faculty and students alike.

Some university professors, like French and Russell, enlist lecture facilitators to support students and teachers in large lecture classes. They discuss this technique in "The Lecture Facilitator: Sorcerer's Apprentice." The facilitators assist with group work, operate the classroom technology, and perform demonstrations. Survey results indicate that students benefited from the use of lecture facilitators. The authors conclude that the use of facilitators made the transition from traditional teaching styles to an inquiry-based style much easier for students and faculty.

Convinced that active learning is more effective than the traditional lecture, Pestel uses "discovery questions" to help develop independent learning in her classes. A description of this technique appears in "Facilitating the Reading/Discussion Connection in the Interactive Classroom." Pestel presents examples of the types of discovery questions she uses. Each question is structured around a specific and limited reading assignment. These questions are distributed at the beginning of class and students are given 10–20 minutes to work in groups to determine the answers.

Writing is a valuable learning tool, but it is difficult to include in many large classes. In their article, "A Peer-Reviewed Research Assignment for Large Classes," Henderson and Buising report on a successful technique they have used to incorporate writing in their classes. They use active learning in collaborative groups to produce research papers on instructor-supplied topics in a biochemistry class. Peer groups evaluate first drafts, and final drafts are posted on a class website for additional evaluation and feedback. Students receive evaluation criteria in advance so they know how to write their papers and how to provide helpful feedback to their peers.

Stencel provides a slightly different method to help make a transition from the didactic lecture approach. His article, "An Interactive Lecture Notebook—Twelve Ways to Improve Students' Grades," presents a strategy on how to draw students' attention to what they need to know in a lecture. Students comment that the interactive notebook helped them get more involved in class and others felt the notebooks gave them time to learn and listen instead of just trying to write notes in class.

A number of professors incorporate the use of modern information technology into their courses to make the classes more interactive. E-mail communication is one of the leading ways to enhance communication between students and instructors. Hedges and Mania-Farnell describe how redirecting students' work through e-mail helped students identify misconceptions and helped the instructor identify areas that needed to be covered further in a human biology class. In "Using E-mail to Improve Communication in the Introductory Science Classroom," the authors describe how students were asked to read a variety of current articles and news briefs from journals and science magazines, and then discuss the articles by e-mail. Besides increased student-instructor interaction, the authors discuss several other beneficial outcomes.

In "Using Internet Class Notes and PowerPoint in the Physical Geology Lecture," Mantei explains how these technologies lead to higher exam scores for students. He compares student performance in physical geology classes using traditional lecture methods and those where lecture notes and practice examinations were placed on a class website. Preliminary evaluation data show strong student acceptance for these techniques.

Marbach-Ad and Sokolove tell how students in a large mixed majors/nonmajors introductory biology class used e-mail and written notes for questions on class content or organization. Their article, "Creating Direct Channels of Communication: Fostering Interaction with E-mail and In-class Notes," indicates that women and science majors were most likely to communicate in this manner. For students who are reluctant to ask questions during class and those having questions outside of class, this method is efficient and effective.

Action research provides a unique way to improve teaching practices. Adams and Slater present their findings in an article titled "Using Action Research to Bring the Large Class Down to Size." They present four action research studies conducted in support of improving introductory astronomy, a course with more than 200 nonscience majors in a single lecture. The article provides readers with evidence that the large-group learning environment can be improved by making decisions based on data.

Another professor used an assessment tool to help refine teaching techniques. In "Gauging Student's Learning in the Classroom: An Assessment Tool to Help Refine Instructors' Teaching Techniques," Heady reports that the use of the Student Assessment of Learning Gains (SALG) in an introductory biology course is a more helpful instrument than traditional course evaluations in obtaining data that can be used to improve course instruction.

In conclusion, professors whose articles are presented in this collection have used the most current research on teaching and learning, information technology, and research to improve large-group instruction at their colleges and universities. The strategies they present range from small-scale innovations to a complete revamping of teaching techniques. The desire to improve college science teaching and learning is the goal of each author. Their strategies provide excellent examples for others who wish to move away from the traditional lecture-only method.

Timothy M. Cooney
NSTA College Division Director
Professor of Earth Science and Science Education
University of Northern Iowa

Innovative Techniques for Large-Group Instruction brings you *sci*LINKS, a new project that blends the two main delivery systems for curriculum—books and telecommunications—into a dynamic new educational tool for children, their parents, and their teachers. *sci*LINKS links specific science content with instructionally rich Internet resources. *sci*LINKS represents an enormous opportunity to create new pathways for learners, new opportunities for professional growth among teachers, and new modes of engagement for parents.

In this *sci*LINKed text, you will find an icon near several of the concepts being discussed. Under it, you will find the *sci*LINKS URL (*www.scilinks.org*) and a code. Go to the *sci*LINKS website, sign in, type the code from your text, and you will receive a list of URLs that are selected by science educators. Sites are chosen for accurate and age-appropriate content and good pedagogy. The underlying database changes constantly, eliminating dead or revised sites or simply replacing them with better selections. The *sci*LINKS search team regularly reviews the materials to which this text points, so you can always count on good content being available.

The selection process involves four review stages:

1. First, a cadre of undergraduate science education majors searches the World Wide Web for interesting science resources. The undergraduates submit about 500 sites a week for consideration.

2. Next, packets of these web pages are organized and sent to teacher-webwatchers with expertise in given fields and grade levels. The teacher-webwatchers can also submit web pages that they have found on their own. The teachers pick the jewels from this selection and correlate them to the National Science Education Standards. These pages are submitted to the *sci*LINKS database.

3. Scientists review these correlated sites for accuracy.

4. NSTA staff approve the web pages and edit the information provided for accuracy and consistent style.

*sci*LINKS is a free service for textbook and supplemental resource users, but obviously someone must pay for it. Participating publishers pay a fee to NSTA for each book that contains *sci*LINKS. The program is also supported by a grant from the National Aeronautics and Space Administration (NASA).

How Do College Students Best Learn Science?

An Assessment of Popular Teaching Styles and Their Effectiveness

William H. Leonard

This paper is based on William Leonard's "How Do College Students Learn Science?" Chapter 1 in *Effective Teaching and Course Management for University and College Science Teachers,* edited by E. Siebert, M. Caprio, and C. Lyda. Dubuque, IA: Kendall/ Hunt Publishing Co.

The vast majority of college students are not successfully learning science. Lord summed it up, "The present way we teach undergraduate science at colleges and universities almost everywhere simply does not stimulate active learning" (1994). The dominant lecture method just does not seem to be doing the job (Leonard 1992).

Our students entering and leaving high school are not scoring well on tests that measure understanding of science (and mathematics) relative to other developed countries, and this appears to continue through college (National Center for Education Statistics 1997). Moreover, college science courses are notorious for poor teaching (Lord 1994; Seymour 1995). In fact, Angelo (1990) has shown that students remember only 20 percent of what they hear in a traditional lecture.

Researchers and educators have suggested that one major reason for

the lack of success of the lecture method is that students do not expend much energy thinking about what is being discussed in a traditional lecture presentation. On the other hand, a truly interactive lecture, interactive group learning, or experiential learning setting such as a laboratory or field work provides plenty of opportunities for students to process, interpret, and internalize the concepts they experience.

The literature contains many testimonials and experimental research studies that support the idea that meaningful learning is tied to experience (Bodner 1986; Leonard 1989 a and b; Angelo 1990; Lorsch and Tobin 1992; Bybee 1993; Caprio 1994; Lawson 1990, 1992, 1993; Lord 1994; Roth 1994 Seymour 1995). Cannon (1999) has suggested that a lack of appropriate learning strategies (especially student-centered methods) is the largest variable contributing to attrition in science majors.

CONSTRUCTIVIST LEARNING

A learning approach called *constructivism* is receiving much attention in the literature. Frequently cited as the source of this term, von Glasserfeld (1987) states, "Constructivism is a theory which asserts that knowledge is not primarily received,

but actively built and that the function of cognition is adaptive and serves the organization of the experiential world." Rooted in Piagetian thought, information processing, and concept mapping, constructivism assumes that learners build upon prior experiences. The learner has a neural network that organizes and relates previously learned knowledge. New understandings are constructed by the learner as a result of new experiences.

"Constructivists hold that learning is an interpretive process, as new information is given meaning in terms of the student's prior knowledge. Each learner actively constructs and reconstructs his or her understanding rather than receiving it from a more authoritative source such as a teacher or textbook" (Roth 1994).

Constructivist learning can be compared or contrasted to an *objectivist* approach in which knowledge is viewed as something that can be imparted. Objectivists like to use the lecture approach because they believe that

William H. Leonard, editor of JCST's "Research and Teaching" department, is a professor of science education and biology at Clemson University, Clemson, SC 29634-0708; e-mail: leonard@clemson.edu.

they can open up the student's head, pour in knowledge, close the student's head and then have the student take a test. Caprio (1994) believes that, "The objectivist teacher rewards students when their understanding is more or less the same as that of the instructor." This is a very dangerous learning approach when viewed in terms of how scientists themselves discover new knowledge. The objectivist approach is also popular among university administrators interested in the lowest possible cost of getting a student through a course.

Constructivist learning has also garnered much support in the literature ranging from philosophical discussions, testimonials by instructors who have seen constructivism work successfully with their students, and experimental studies showing higher student performance in constructivist learning environments (Bodner 1986; von Glasserfeld 1987; Lawson 1988; Braathen and Hewson 1988; Tobin 1990; Leonard 1991; Yeany and Britton 1991; Harris and Marks 1992; Lawson 1988, 1992; Lorsbach and Tobin 1992; Bybee 1993; Leonard and Penick 1993; Caprio 1994; Glynn and Lord 1994; Pressley, Harris, and Marks 1992; Seymour 1995; Leonard and Penick 1998; Leonard, Penick, and Speziale 1999; and Cannon 1999).

Lord has suggested that having students work in collaborative groups is central to a constructivist learning environment because it provides opportunities for students to clarify their understandings.

Constructivism warrants serious consideration in college science teaching. It is becoming clearer to many college science faculty that constructivism facilitates meaningful understanding of science. The strong support in the literature for constructivism is probably why both the *National Science Education Standards* and the *Benchmarks for Science Literacy* endorse constructivist approaches to learning.

STUDENTS LEARN IN DIFFERENT WAYS

There is also much evidence that students learn in different ways. The term *learning styles* has been used extensively in the literature to describe the possible means by which an individual student may best learn. Some research supports that individuals prefer to learn through one or more of the different senses (Jung 1970). Concrete learners rely more on touch, taste, and smell and more intuitive and abstract learners prefer hearing and sight.

Meyers and Briggs (1958) believe that learning style preferences are related to personality type. For example, sensory learners (S) depend on experiences taken in through their senses. Intuitive learners (I) benefit from discussions of abstractions. Feeling learners (F) tend to relate what they learn to their own personal and/or societal values. Thinking learners (T) benefit most from a logical progression of organized and related concepts.

There is also evidence to suggest that the vast majority of learners do not sort entirely into any one of the above categories but instead into four combinations of two of these categories (Silver, Hansen, and Strong 1981; Krause 1996). Thus, ST (sensory-thinking) learners need a highly organized and quiet environment, work best alone, memorize well, benefit from repetitive drill and practice and do well on recall exams.

Krause (1996) believes that STs are the classic student for which American schools have been structured. The SF (sensory-feeling) is a verbal learner, is highly interpersonal, and benefits from stories and examples. Cooperative learning works well for SFs. ST and SF

An experiential learning setting such as this laboratory at Clemson University provides plenty of opportunities for students to process, interpret, and internalize the concepts they learn.

learners are a large proportion of entering college freshmen. They are highly constructivist because they build abstractions through progressive concrete experiences.

IT (intuitive-thinking) learners search for logic and patterns of understanding. Since it is beneficial for them to see the whole picture of where specific knowledge fits, advance organizers such as concept maps are helpful. Being global and deductive learners, they do not memorize well but can handle abstract theories. IF (intuitive-feeling) learners tend to learn from metaphors, do well in social contexts such as cooperative learning, yet are very creative. Krause (1996) believes that that IF learners are the most endangered in traditional American schools.

There is much debate in the literature on learning styles primarily because of the different ways in which learning styles are categorized. Some evidence indicates that learning is most effective if a student is provided information about his or her unique learning style preference and is then given instruction that takes into account that particular style (Krause 1996). It has been suggested that most instructors teach using their own preferred learning style and overlook the fact that most of the students in their class learn better in other ways. Given that there do seem to be style preferences in the way individuals learn, instructors may be well advised to first recognize this and then try to diversify the teaching methods they use in order to accommodate the learning needs of a diverse student population.

RECOMMENDATIONS

▲ *Use significantly more active learning.* Active learning is already a large part of contemporary high school science curricula, discussed in such texts as *ChemCom: Chemistry in the Community* (1998), *Biology: A Community*

Context (1988), and *Active Physics* (1998). Active learning is also emerging in mathematics, language arts, and social studies curricula because it makes learning interesting to teachers and students alike. It also provides learning based upon experiences to which students can make relevant connections to their worlds.

The college science community

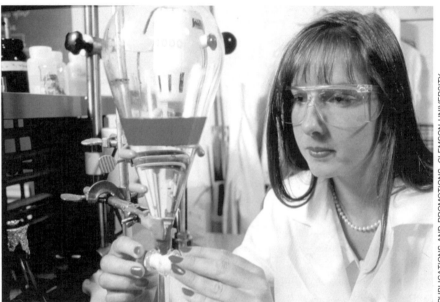

A science student in a Clemson University lab. Professor Leonard recommends teaching science concepts in lab before the lecture so students' learning proceeds from concrete to abstract.

should examine these constructivist and standards-based curricula as possible models for future college science textbooks. Because of the characteristics of the majority of students taking our science courses, an active-learning environment is the most appropriate mode of instruction

▲ *Implement constructivist learning environments in your classroom.* The many ways to do this in college science courses are now appearing regularly in the literature, especially in *JCST*. Suggestions for asking questions in large enrollment lecture courses to promote inquiry have been outlined (Leonard 1992). This "reverse-lecture" approach

was found to be more interesting to students than the old-fashioned lecture because there is an element of mystery as well as more active student participation in the learning process. The interaction between instructor and student provides students time to adequately process concepts.

Lawson (1992) has suggested some specific ways to "push" previously transitional and concrete thinkers into understanding formal concepts when given a progression of concrete to formal experiences with the concepts. The notion that formal operations are somewhat experiential and contextual has important implications for college science instruction. More college science curricula, which are able to do this, need to be explored and developed.

Lord (1994) tells how he uses Bybee's (1993) 5E constructivist model (engage, explore, explain, elaborate, and evaluate) to improve student interaction in large group biology courses. Caprio (1994) describes how he lectured less and gave students more responsibility outside of class for their own learning. Cannon (1999) suggests assessing the student perception of the extent to which a classroom environment is consistent with constructivist epistemology. He has developed an instrument that can help teachers to reflect on and, perhaps, reshape their teaching practices.

▲ *Use lab before lecture to teach the same science concepts.* This allows instruction to proceed from concrete to abstract and will make learning much more successful for nonmajor students.

▲ *Provide your students with a conceptual framework and advance organizers.* Advance organizers allow ideas to fit into students' existing networks and will encourage students to relate what is being learned to what is already known.

▲ *Accommodate the many ways in which different students learn by using many different approaches.* In two articles published in 1989, I made suggestions for accommodating different student learning styles using visuals and objects and for making abstractions more concrete to students in large-enrollment classes.

▲ *Use science content and instructional methods consistent with the National Science Education Standards and Benchmarks for Science Literacy.* Bybee and McInerney (1995) recommend that colleges and universities implement national standards and benchmarks both in their courses for nonmajors and in their teacher preparation programs. In addition, they recommend that colleges and universities use appropriate, research-based pedagogy for these audiences. These recommendations include science department programs that train teaching assistants. ■

References

American Association for the Advancement of Science. 1993. *Benchmarks for Science Literacy.* New York: Oxford University Press.

Angelo, T. A. 1990. *Learning in the Classroom (Phase I).* A report from the Lawrence Hall of Science. Berkeley, CA: University of California.

Bodner, G. M. 1986. Constructivism: A theory of knowledge. *Journal of Chemical Education* 63:873-878.

Braathen, P. C., and P. W. Hewson. 1988. A case study of prior knowledge, learning approach and conceptual change in an introductory college chemistry tutorial program. ERIC Accession # ED292687.

BSCS. 1993. *Developing Biological Literacy.* Boulder, CO: Biological Sciences Curriculum Study.

Bybee, R. 1993. An instructional model for science education. In *Developing Biological Literacy.* Colorado Spring, CO: Biological Sciences Curriculum Study.

Bybee, R., and J. McInerney. 1995. *Redesigning the Science Curriculum.* Colorado Springs, CO: BSCS.

Cannon, J. 1999. Cooperating with constructivism. *Journal of College Science Teaching* 29 (1): 17-23.

Caprio, M. W. 1994. Easing into constructivism. *Journal of College Science Teaching* 23:210-212.

Eisenkraft, A., R. Hobbie, J. Koser, T. Goerke, and T. Lee. 1998. *Active Physics.* Amonk, NY: IT'S ABOUT TIME.

Glynn, S. M., R. H. Yeany, and B. K. Britton. 1991. A constructive view of learning science. In *The Psychology of Learning Science,* eds. S.M. Glynn et al., 3-20. Hillsdale, NJ: Lawrence Erlbaum Associates.

Jung, C. G. 1970. *Analytical Psychology, Its Theory and Practice.* New York: Vintage Books (original work published in 1936).

Krause, L. B. 1996. *An investigation of learning styles in general chemistry students.* Ph.D. Dissertation, Clemson University, Clemson, SC.

Lawson, A. E. 1988. A better way to teach biology. *American Biology Teacher* 50:266-273.

Lawson, A. E. 1992. The development of reasoning among college biology students: A review of research. *Journal of College Science Teaching* 22:338-344.

Leonard, W. H. 1988. What Research Says about Biology Laboratory Instruction. *American Biology Teacher* 50:303-306.

Leonard, W. H. 1989a. Ten years of research on science laboratory instruction at the college level. *Journal of College Science Teaching* 18:303-306.

Leonard, W. H. 1989b. Using inquiry laboratory strategies in college science courses. Research matters . . . to the science teacher. *National Association for Research in Science Teaching* 24:1-2.

Leonard, W. H. 1989c. Problems with large group instruction: What can we do? Paper presented to the Society of College Science Teachers, NSTA National Convention in Seattle.

Leonard, W. H. 1992. Lecturing using inquiry. Paper presented to the Society for College Science Teaching, National Science Teachers National Convention in Boston.

Leonard, W. H., and J. E. Penick. 1993. What's important in selecting a biology text? *American Biology Teacher* 55:14-19.

Leonard, W., and J. Penick. 1998. *Biology: A Community Context.* Cincinnati, OH: South-Western Educational Publishing/ITP.

Leonard, W., J. Penick, and B. Speziale. 1999. Performance assessment of a standards-based high school biology curriculum. Paper presented to the Annual Meeting of the National Association for Research in Science Teaching, Boston, March 29.

Lord, T. 1994. Using constructivism to enhance student learning in college biology. *Journal of College Science Teaching* 23:346-348.

Lorsbach, A., and K. Tobin. 1992. Research Matters . . . To the science teacher: Constructivism as a referent for science teaching. *NARST Monograph* 5:21-27.

Meyers, I., and M. McCaulley. 1958. *Manual: A Guide to the Development and Use of the Myers-BriggsType Type Indictor.* Palo Alto, CA: Consulting Psychologists Press.

National Center for Educational Statistics. 1997. *A Study of Eighth-Grade Mathematics and Science Teaching, Learning, Curriculum and Achievement in International Contexts.* Washington, D.C.: U.S. Department of Education.

National Research Council. 1996. *National Science Education Standards.* Washington, D.C.: National Academy Press.

Novak, J. 1991. Clarify with concept maps. *Science Teacher* 58:44-49.

Pressley, M., R. K. Harris, and M. B. Marks. 1992. But good strategy instructors are constructivists. *Educational Psychology Review* 4:3-31.

Roth, W-M.. 1994. Experimenting in a constructivist high school physics laboratory. *Journal of Research in Science Teaching* 31(2): 189-223.

Rutherford, F. J., and A. Algren. 1990. *Science for All Americans.* New York: Oxford University Press.

Seymour, E. 1995. Revisiting the problem iceberg: Science, mathematics and engineering students still chilled out. *Journal of College Science Teaching* 24:392-400.

Silver, H., and J. R. Hansen. 1981. *Teaching Styles and Strategies.* Moorestown, NJ: Hanson Silver Strong and Accociates, Inc.

Stanitski, C., and P. Smith. 1998. *ChemCom: Chemistry in the Community.* Dubuque, IA: Kendall/ Hunt Publishing Co.

Tobin, K. 1990. Research on science laboratory activities: In pursuit of better questions and answers to improve learning. *School Science and Mathematics* 90:403-418.

Von Glasserfeld, E. 1987. Learning as a constructive activity. In *Problems of Representation in the Teaching and Learning of Mathematics*, ed. C. Janvier. Hillsdale, NJ: Lawrence Erlbaum Associates

Are We Cultivating 'Couch Potatoes' in Our College Science Lectures?

Weeding Out the Bad Teaching Habits That Inhibit Students' Growth

Thomas R. Lord

At a recent annual meeting of marketing executives in New York City, the nationally known keynote speaker announced to the audience that *couch potato* television watchers outnumber their *noncouch potato* counterparts by almost two to one.

To earn the distinction of being a couch potato, the speaker continued, two things were necessary. First, a couch potato candidate had to watch more than 25 hours of TV a week (an amount reached by over 78 percent of the American public). More importantly, during the time the viewer is watching television, his or her attention to specifics can be no more than 50 percent of his or her capacity.

The speaker's reason for providing the information was to make the point that, in today's highly competitive commercial marketplace, promotional advertising need not be overly detailed to convince consumers to purchase the product.

Sometimes I feel today's students are more like couch potatoes than ardent learners. I recall visiting a colleague who, several years earlier, had left my college to take a position at a large research university. I arrived at his institution just as his mid-morning general biology class was about to be-

> *Professors shouldn't cover the content for their students; rather, they should uncover it.*

gin. Noting the time, he invited me to take a seat in the back of the lecture hall to "soak in" his lecture. I decided to take him up on his invitation and found an empty chair in the center of the last row of the theater.

As I sat there, the hall quickly filled with undergraduates. I was struck by the fact that most of the students seemed semi-awake as they moved toward the same swing-out arm chairs they had taken since the first day of class. Once seated, they pulled tattered notebooks from their unzipped backpacks and stationed them on their desks. With notebooks in place, the students comfortably waited for the lecture to begin.

As my friend was about to speak, a few students entered the room more lethargic then their classmates and maneuvered in my direction to the back of the lecture hall. There they lowered

themselves into the few remaining unoccupied seats, skipped the backpack part of the ritual, and awaited the professor's opening words.

By then my colleague was in place behind a lectern and next to a large chalkboard in the front of the hall. As he began his lecture I could hear the scrawl of pencils and the whirl of paper as students prepared to take notes. Besides these sounds and the jawing gum-chewers in front of me, the presenter's voice was the only other sound in the room. The students dutifully sat scribbling notes onto their pads: no one disrupted the presentation, no one raised a hand, and no one questioned their role in the learning process.

About 20 minutes into the lecture the mood was interrupted when the teacher interjected a humorous, personal experience into his presentation. The event redirected the class's focus from the notebooks to the professor, and mild laughter and talking arose from the gallery. For a few short min-

Thomas Lord is a professor of biology at Indiana University of Pennsylvania, 114 Weynandt Hall, Indiana, PA 15705-1090; e-mail: TRLORD@ GROVE.IUP.EDU.

utes, my colleague had regained the students' attention, but it was short-lived, and the atmosphere quickly returned to the previous quiet as he returned to his prescriptive delivery.

Forty minutes into the lecture I looked around the room: a handful of kids were still frantically taking notes, several students were copying the terms that the professor had earlier written on the chalkboard, and a few were sleeping or reading the college newspaper, but most of the students were just sitting quietly. Despite their opened eyes, their stares were unfocused and their faces held no expression. These students reminded me of the passive couch potatoes the marketing conference speaker had described.

The students remained that way for a while longer when suddenly the activity level picked up in the room. The eyes of the students refocused as they took control of their postures, and I immediately realized the reason for the change. My colleague had asked if there were any questions about what he had presented during the hour. Despite their now attentive frame of mind, no questions were raised by the audience and the class ended. Students stuffed their pencils and notebooks into their backpacks, grabbed their jackets, and moved out of the lecture hall.

I got up, and walked to the front to join my friend as he stuffed the last page of his lecture into his attaché case. Noticing me approach, he asked if I'd like to join him for a lunch at his expense. Since I never turn down an invitation for a free meal, we adjourned to the faculty dining room of the university.

Over lunch, my friend conveyed how proud he was of the modifications he had made with the course I had witnessed. During the previous summer he had spent several weeks adding new, cutting-edge findings to every course topic and had (in his words) "brought the course up to the twenty-first cen-

tury." Then, with a inquisitive expression on his face, he asked what I thought of the class I had just seen.

A long time went by before I answered. I didn't want to tell him that his students didn't pay much attention during the lecture and that they probably didn't learn a great deal, but I couldn't tell him what he expected to hear either. "I'm sorry Jack, what did you say?" I asked, stalling for time and hoping something would come to me.

"What did you think of my lecture?" he reiterated. Again it seemed like minutes passed as my mind searched for a response. Nothing came to me, but I realized that I had to answer his question: "You're sure giving your students a challenging science course," I blurted and congratulated him on his grasp of the difficult content. Before he could respond, I quickly added, "What do you think of this university's fringe benefit package?" I managed to avoid discussing my colleague's teaching for the rest of my visit.

As I drove back to my college later that day, I wondered why science professors are so reluctant to give up the old lecture method of teaching. Surely professors who follow the practice realize that, despite their attendance, the students aren't putting much effort into the learning process. And when the students *are* listening, most of them are too busy scribbling notes to think about the substance of the lecture.

Another friend, who teaches at a university in Great Britain, jokingly refers to this common practice in American higher education as the "sponge and liquid" principle of teaching. "Every time an American professor enters the class," he would say, "he carries with him a pouch full of irrefutable content as if it were some kind of astute liquid. During the delivery, the professor casts the liquid throughout the lecture hall, sometimes in sprinkles and other times in torrents. As this happens, sponges (the students)

roll about the room in an attempt to absorb as much of the liquid as they possibly can before it evaporates (I wish my students were as active). But the sponges are not all the same."

My English friend added, "[The sponges] are of different shapes, sizes, and absorptive potentials. Large, pliable sponges have an easier time of soaking up the liquid than small, pliable sponges, but quickly moving small sponges can soak up more liquid than slow moving large ones. So there is not only the problem of acquiring the critical information before it evaporates, but there's the complication of all the other sponges getting in the way.

"The continuous and constant competition for the information," continued my British colleague, "creates a learning environment that is neither healthy nor supportive. By mid-term, most of the sponges (especially those that find the fluid distasteful anyway) give up rolling in the liquid and exert only enough effort to remain moist until the course ends. Furthermore, many of the sponges suited for this method of teaching also tire of the competition and join their dampened companions."

Many science professors consider "sponge and liquid" lecturing to be the only way to teach at the college level. After all, lecturing does let the students know exactly what the professor thinks is important and what will likely appear on the exams. Lecturing seems to be the easiest way to teach science; it's easily adapted to different audiences and time frames, and it allows the professor to constantly remain the focus of the class.

I wondered if lecturing in science really could do more harm than good to student learning. The more I thought about it, the more convinced I became that it could, for these reasons:

▲ Lecturing is based on the assumption that all college students have the same level of background knowledge on the science topic. Lectures can waste the better students' time by covering things that they already know or can easily read for themselves. Lectures for the weaker student, however, usually bring on frustration and disinterest (Brown et al. 1989).

▲ Science lectures are always given at the same pace. Educational theorists tell us, however, that college students learn science at a variety of paces; some are very quick at grasping concepts while others need time to mull over the content before they understand it (Kulik and Kulik 1979).

▲ Science lectures are always presented verbally despite the fact that many of today's students are either strong visual learners or are heavily dependent on manipulatives or other hands-on exploratory activities for their learning (Johnson et al. 1991).

▲ Most college students don't feel comfortable asking questions during lectures and exit the class with misconceptions and incorrect understandings that they have not identified (Stone 1970; Bowers 1986).

▲ And, finally, the level of scientific knowledge gained by students from lectures tends to be low-level, factual content and not the high-level critical thinking and problem solving forms of learning sought in higher education (Bligh 1997; Gabbert et al. 1986; Ruggiero 1988).

But what could science instructors use to replace the lecture? Professors just can't show video movies or assign readings each time students gather for class. As I continued to drive, I continued to think about this when a highway billboard caught my attention. The sign showed a cluster of young adults in thoughtful pose around a small table. In the hand of each person was a bottle of chilled beer

Prof. Thomas Lord, author of this article, teaching biology at Indiana University of Pennsylvania. Prof. Lord has changed his teaching style to encourage students to become active participants in their learning.

while on the table small pine blocks were strewn around a complicated wooden puzzle. The boldface message proclaimed: PENNSY BEER, FOUND WHERE IMPORTANT DISCOVERIES IN LIFE ARE BEING MADE.

As I read the sign I thought about how people discover and learn in real life and quickly concluded that most folks learn through inquiry, basing the new understandings on what they already know. Sometimes they're able to

do this without help, but most of the time men and women collaborate with their friends and coworkers. People learn as they try to figure out questions, puzzles, statements, and other challenges. They launch new learning from their existing knowledge base and can usually be most successful at doing so by collaborating with others.

Instructors, therefore, shouldn't lecture students to supply them with facts to memorize and store for later reference. Instead, the professor's job is to provide challenging experiences and problems that students try to solve based on what they already know. As they figure things out, they learn and build higher levels of knowledge in their minds.

Rather than finding the solution in their textbook or study guide, students should be encouraged to develop their own solutions based on questions the teacher provides. In addition, instructors need to give students the chance to discuss with others and incorporate new understandings and insights. Professors shouldn't *cover the content* for their students; rather, they should *uncover* it.

As my drive home ended, I pulled into a parking lot at my college and found that I had convinced myself that I needed to change my way of teaching science. I knew my students were not learning as much as they could. I knew I could be a more effective teacher and better instill a respect for science in my students. But most of all, I knew I could no longer continue to give my teacher-centered lectures and cultivate couch potatoes in my classes. ∎

References

Bligh, D. A. 1997. *What's the Use of Lectures.* Harmondsworth, England: Penguin.

Bowers, J. 1986. Classroom communication apprehension. *Communication Education* 35(4): 372-378.

Brown, J., A. Collins, and P. Duguid. 1989. Situated cognition and the culture of learning. *Educational Researcher* 18(1): 32-42.

Gabbert, B., D. Johnson, and R. Johnson. 1987. Cooperative learning, groups-to-individual transfer, process gain and the acquisition of cognitive reasoning strategies. *Journal of Psychology* 120(3): 265-278.

Johnson, D., R. Johnson, and K. Smith. 1991. *Active Learning: Cooperation in the College Classroom.* Edina, MN: Interaction Book Company.

Kulik, J., and C. Kulik. 1979. College teaching. In *Research on Teaching: Concepts, Findings and Implications*, eds. P.L. Peterson and H.J. Walberg. Berkeley, CA: McCutcheon.

McKeachie W. 1988. Teaching thinking. *Update* 2(1): 1.

Ruggiero, V. 1988. *Teaching Thinking Across the Curriculum.* New York: Harper & Row.

Stone, E. 1970. Students' attitudes to the size of teaching groups. *Educational Review* 21(2): 98-108.

Getting There from Here

Making the Transition from Traditional Teaching Practices to Those That Are Student Centered

M. W. Caprio and Lynda B. Micikas

An often-told story begins with a confused traveler stopping to ask for directions from a wise old farmer with a wry sense of humor. The motorist has wandered into the back country of one state or another—the story appears in many versions—having exhausted all possibilities of self-help. As expected, the traveler is entirely at the mercy of the local expert.

The farmer clearly knows of the traveler's desired destination and, at first, seems able to direct him there. He begins to give the directions. However, each time he stops part way through, abandons the explanation, and begins anew. Finally, after several false starts, he removes his straw hat, wipes his brow, and scratches his head pensively. He has confused even himself. Then he looks into the eyes of the stranger for a moment, shakes his head slowly, and with a very serious expression, says, "Well, come to think of it, my friend, you just can't get there from here."

When the confused traveler is a college science teacher moving from traditional teaching practices to active learning methods in education, a point

M. W. Caprio, the column editor of JCST's "Two-Year College" department, teaches biology at Volunteer State Community College, 1480 Nashville Pike, Gallatin, TN 37066-3188. Lynda B. Micikas is a senior staff associate and assistant director of the Biological Sciences Curriculum Study, 5415 Mark Dabling Blvd., Colorado Springs, CO 80918-3842.

frequently arrives in the transition when it seems that "you just can't get there from here." The reality, however, is that others have already made the journey and they have brought back some excellent directions.

Moving from a lecture format to one that is more student centered is a difficult step, and there are several reasons for the reluctance invariably felt by teachers who are contemplating the move. The barriers seem to come in two forms. First, there is the "why-should-I?" obstacle. This is the most basic hurdle to reform and arises from the view that we are, after all, good lecturers; we enjoy lecturing, our students pass courses when we lecture at them, and we have all those wonderful "class-tested" lecture notes. So why change? We offer a nonstandard answer to that question below.

Second, there is the "why-I-should-not" obstacle. This barrier to reform is more complex than the first and includes a whole set of reasons that range from excuses in the name of coverage and logistics to very real concerns. We discuss this second barrier to reform in the next section.

WHY SHOULD I GO THERE?

Why should one change to more student centered approaches for teaching introductory college science courses? Sound educational reasons exist to explain why, and pedagogues are out in droves proclaiming them to the masses. Indeed, it would be difficult—perhaps impossible—to attend a meet-ing of science teachers without hearing educational researchers celebrate the new methods and urge their adoption in classrooms. Their explanations are the standard responses to the question of *why change?*, and you can read about them in literature (Caprio, 1994; Leonard, 1997; Lord, 1996; SCST, 1993; Yager, 1991).

But what we promised you here were less conventional reasons, of which we offer two. They are also important, and together with the pedagogical support for reform, they make a compelling case for change.

The first reason is simply that student-centered teaching is fun. Students find it fun, as do teachers. For the teacher, one kind of fun comes in the satisfaction of seeing learning in action. During lectures, we deliver the material, but students learn it elsewhere, in our absence. Of course, that happens when we use active teaching and learning strategies, too. Now, however, teachers have daily opportunities to see their students become involved with the course material, with each other, and with them. The excitement of learning is very evident during these interactions. Teachers find themselves smiling a lot as their students discover the subject matter and construct its meaning for themselves. When we work this way with our students we really feel we are teaching, because we witness learning happening directly before us and we know we play a role in catalyzing it. This is enormously satisfying and rather fun, too.

Student centered teaching brings with it another kind of fun. Educators often describe lecturing as a passive experience for students. But in the words "for students" is implied an active experience for instructors. We are not entirely sure of that. The instructor does prepare the lecture, which involves interaction with the subject matter. In the classroom, however, the teacher is not working with the ideas of science so much as practicing public speaking, while students are mostly engaged in transcription. Sad to say, but in the time they spend together, neither is doing much thinking about science, except in a superficial way. Switch to an active learning strategy, though, and all that changes. Now both instructor and students are grappling with the ideas of science together. They are thinking and asking questions. They are talking about science with one another and with the teacher. And that really is fun.

Perhaps it is not very scholarly to suggest "fun" as a reason for using a particular approach to teaching. But to not seek ways to bring the excitement and pleasure of discussing science to one's classroom is to belie the very reason we chose to do and teach science. We picked the profession because we enjoy teaching. If we fail to offer opportunities for our students to experience this type of pleasure, we conceal from them the power of science to realize intellectual fulfillment. In fact, using student-centered strategies—capitalizing on the fun of thinking and talking about science—allows us to more easily address the difficult domain of effective teaching goals, yet another argument for lecturing less.

A second reason for using student-centered teaching strategies is that these approaches make students partners in the teaching and learning processes. These strategies involve more students, more frequently and more deeply, in the process of learning. *All* students, not just the few who normally contribute to

class discussions, participate in class, at a deeper level and more successfully. In fact, we have never seen a student fall asleep during an active learning session (one of us has actually heard a student snoring during what was a truly magnificent lecture), and class attendance is noticeably better. Transcription can happen whether a student attends class or not; learning, when the central result of having poured over the course content with other students and the instructor, cannot take place if a student is absent. Students quickly figure this out, and come to class because there is no easy substitute for what they gain by being present.

Acknowledging that students are

For the teacher, Mario Caprio, Two-Year College column editor, fun comes in the satisfaction of seeing learning in action.

partners in the teaching and learning process may also yield other rewards. The ultimate responsibility for learning has always resided with the students; if the students do not master the coursework, they and not the teacher suffer the consequences. This is implicit in all college courses. Student-centered approaches make the students' responsibility explicit and provide them with the tools, resources, and support they need to meet that responsibility. In this learning environment, they also have the opportunity

to employ learning models similar to the ones used in the working world, where the responsibility for learning rests clearly on the individual.

WHY I SHOULD NOT GO THERE

The case for active learning strategies—the answer to the "why-should-I" obstacle—is so strong that only the most formidable barrier could prohibit its acceptance. But for many of us, another important impediment exists: the various reasons each of us can give for "why I should not." We must identify these reasons and distinguish the real ones from those with less substance.

Of the latter (with the risk of alienating a few readers, we can call them *excuses*), we hear two most often. The first is the concern that active learning strategies make it impossible to "cover" the content listed in the syllabus. In fact, actual classroom experience and rigorous educational research has disproved this argument (Caprio, 1994; Bonwell and Eison, 1991). Many active learning strategies are comparable to lectures in promoting mastery of content. They are even superior to lectures in promoting the development of students' thinking, speaking, and writing skills. Once students develop these important learning skills, they can assume more responsibility for learning content on their own.

The second excuse claims that these methods are not appropriate for large classes. However, many ways exist to bring effective active learning experiences into a large lecture hall. Consider, for example, this passage from a recent monograph published by the Society for College Science Teachers:

Most of my teaching is, as it was, in huge rooms with hundreds of students in them. (Sigh.) But my teaching strategies have expanded way beyond the lecture. This past semester I conducted 340 students who have performed their own symphony of science. We did hands-on, "laboratory" exercises, in a room that holds 400 people sitting in chairs bolted to the floor. Architects designed those rooms for lecturing, but you can turn them into other kinds of teaching spaces. One day groups of my students were blowing up balloons in order to understand how the universe expands. Another day, they were dunking plastic drink bottles in baggies filled with ice to explore the dependence of temperature on pressure (Shipman, 1997).

Peter Frederick (1987) describes five areas where active learning can occur in large classes.

Other "why-I-should-not" concerns, which are very real, might if unaddressed, lead us to *reject* the arguments for using student-centered strategies in our classrooms. These concerns have one very important element in common: they all evolve from our commitment to offer our best to our students. None of us wants to provide less than our best effort, and if we lecture well, it seems risky to abandon that approach for new techniques with which we feel less secure.

So how do we handle these concerns? One approach is simply to look at them carefully. If we can better understand them, we might be able to find reasonable ways around them. We discuss two potential and closely related concerns below, and then consider some ways to "get there from here," these problems notwithstanding.

One concern, not often expressed by faculty but perhaps often felt, is that *in a traditional lecture, the lecturer controls virtually everything about the class meeting.* For the most part, this is how it was when we were students. We sat in lecture sections where, in addition to science, we learned about teaching. Our professors were our models. So when we were deciding whether to pursue teaching careers, we matched our personalities against our teachers, and when we started to teach, theirs was the model we emulated.

In addition, we expected teaching to put us in control at the "head of the class" when we signed our first teaching contracts. We were comfortable with that role; it is a secure position to hold. It is secure because we know how

to make things work when we lecture and how to respond when the unexpected happens. We know we can look and feel successful with this approach. Now, though, someone is suggesting that we switch from a teacher-centered to a student-centered classroom and relinquish some of that security. The tension this suggestion produces comes from the struggle between the emotional self, who would rather stay safe in that familiar comfort zone of what we can control, and, thus, do well, and the rational self, who recognizes the overwhelming evidence validating the new methods (*e.g.*, Angelo, 1993; Weiss, 1992; Whitman, 1988).

A second personal concern about reform, also rarely expressed but often felt, is closely related to the first. The reality is that *many of us do not know how to teach any other way.* Most college science teachers have had no formal education in how to teach. We have learned primarily by examples passed on from our teachers, and those examples have almost exclusively been minor variations on the lecture model. Such a system for training college teachers promotes traditionalism and does not easily admit new developments. Now that the cognitive sciences have added so much to what we know about how people learn, the traditional lecture approach seems stultifying. But where are college teachers to turn to revitalize their classroom techniques? And how are we to gain sufficient experience with new approaches to become as comfortable in front of the podium as behind it?

SO HOW DO WE GET THERE FROM HERE?

However rationally you may approach change, the decision to adopt active learning strategies carries some emotional implications. The reality need not be as difficult as we expect it to be. If you are lucky, someone in your department may have already started to travel this way, and may

share some direction and companionship with you. But if that is not the case, or you just prefer to begin on your own, how do you get started?

First, understand that although some may visualize student-centered approaches as bringing anarchy into the classroom, that is not really the case. The instructor is still in control, but the control is more subtle. The students may have more freedom to explore the content of our courses, and they are definitely on a much longer leash than they are in a lecture setting, but they are still on a leash, and the instructor still guides them through the subject matter. The techniques of classroom management are more democratic than they are in the lecture hall, but they are effective nonetheless. Welty provides some useful examples of management strategies (1989).

Second, and perhaps more importantly, remember that this is *not* an all-or-nothing situation. You are not required to totally abandon what you are doing now. Lecturing can be extremely effective when used in combination with some of these techniques, and it is a simple matter to introduce brief, student-centered teaching methods into a lecture setting. Furthermore, if you ease into them at a comfortable rate, your classroom management skills will grow proportionately as you develop the methodology. Rushing into these methods—as would be true for any new, nontrivial challenge—is a sure road to failure. Be gentle with yourself. Move slowly.

Third, make use of the many resources around you for help, support, and encouragement. As we said before, others have already made the journey and have brought back some excellent directions.

Peer coaching is one excellent resource. Although it goes by several names, it is essentially a one-on-one relationship where two teachers help one another expand and deepen their pedagogical expertise. It often focuses on a particular classroom issue. Sometimes one of the teachers is the avowed expert, but usually the relationship is between equals, as its name implies. Some schools have peer coaching programs, where the coaches have been specially trained to do this sort of work; in other cases, the process is more informal.

Professional development centers are becoming a more common sight at colleges. These centers also may be called teaching and learning centers, teacher centers, staff development centers, or teaching resource rooms. Their function is to help teachers hone their craft, usually with a "teachers-helping-teachers" approach. The staff at these centers tend to be very responsive to faculty needs and interests. Expressing interest in learning more about student-centered techniques will surely be met with an answer, usually in the form of a workshop.

Professional societies are another source of professional development in student-centered teaching strategies. Attending presentations at meetings of the National Science Teachers Association, the Society for College Science Teachers, and/or one of the teaching societies in the science subdisciplines will yield an enormous amount of information about what others are doing in this area. This venue is especially valuable for faculty who find that *they* are the innovators on their campuses and have no one at home to look to for leadership.

The literature offers a wide range of advice and direction for the would-be reformer. In the "Two-Year College" column last May, one of us, under the pressure of three simultaneous deadlines, squirmed out of this column's deadline by writing about the things on which he was working (Caprio, 1997a). Those other two publications also described various projects. One, the SCST monograph, contains 14 papers in which colleagues describe the barriers they encountered as they moved toward innovation and how they overcame them (Caprio, 1997b). The other is a handbook for new teachers to help them begin their careers as constructivists in education, as well as for the more experienced teachers who wish to break (or, perhaps, modify) the old molds (Seibert, *et al.*, 1997).

We recently discovered an excellent text in the proceedings of an NSF-sponsored conference on inquiry approaches to science teaching held at Hampshire College, in June 1996 (McNeal and D'Avanzo, 1997). All of these resources have extensive bibliographies and all of them discuss practical classroom techniques that we do not have the space to describe here.

Finally, remember that active learning approaches to teaching are independent of subject matter and grade level. That may sound strange, but it is true. These methods go to the heart of how people learn. The techniques that work in science classes also work in English classes, and methods used at the elementary level can work in advanced courses, too.

The sad truth is that when it comes to student-centered approaches to teaching, college science teachers are among the last to join the movement. Elementary, middle, and high schools have been in this mode for some time now. Undergraduate English classes we sat in many years ago were already student-centered and were not even considered especially innovative for their time. We must not overlook opportunities to learn from *all* our colleagues.

Help is out there and it is accessible. Ask directions. You *can* get there from here. ∎

References

Angelo, T.A. 1993. A "teacher's dozen": Fourteen general research-based principles for improving higher learning in our classrooms. *AAHE Bulletin* 45(8): 3–7.

Bonwell, C.C., and J.A. Eison. 1991. Active learning: Creating Excitement in the Classroom. *ASHE-ERIC Higher Education Report No. 1.* Washington: D.C. The George Washington University, School of Education and Human Development.

Caprio, M.W. 1994. Easing into constructivism. *Journal for College Science Teaching* 23(1).

Caprio, M.W. 1997a. Bits and pieces: A glance at some of SCST's future publications. *The Journal for College Science Teaching* 26(6): 439-440.

Caprio, M.W., ed. 1997b. *The SCST Monograph Series: From Traditional Approaches Toward Innovation.* Greenville, SC: Society for College Science Teachers.

Frederick, Peter J. 1987. Student involvement: Active learning in large classes, teaching large classes well. In *New Directions of Teaching and Learning,* 45-56. San Francisco: Jossey-Bass.

Halyard, R. 1993. Introductory college-level science courses: The SCST position statement. *Journal of College Science Teaching* 23(1): 29-30.

Leonard, William H. 1997. How do college students learn science? In *Effective Teaching and Course Management for University and College Science Teachers,* ed. E. Siebert, M. Caprio, and C. Lyda. Dubuque, IA: Kendall/Hunt Publishing Co.

Lord, T. 1996. A comparison between traditional and constructivist teaching in college biology. *Innovative Higher Education* 21(3).

McNeal, A.P., and C. D'Avanzo, eds. 1997. *Student-Active Science: Models of Innovation in College Science Teaching.* New York, NY: Saunders College Publishing.

Shipman, Harry L. 1997. Not just a lecturer anymore. In *The SCST Monograph Series: From Traditional Approaches Toward Innovation,* ed. M. W. Caprio. Greenville, SC: Society for College Science Teachers.

Siebert, E., M. Caprio, C. Lyda, eds. 1997. *Introductory Science Courses: Teaching and Classroom Management.* Dubuque, IA: Kendall/Hunt.

Weiss, C.A. 1992. But how do we get them to think? *Teaching Excellence* 4(5): 1–2.

Welty, W.M. 1989. Discussion method teaching: A practical guide. *To Improve the Academy* 8:197–216.

Whitman, N.A. 1988. Peer teaching: To teach is to learn twice. *ASHE-ERIC Higher Education Reports No. 4.* Washington, D.C.: Association for the Study of Higher Education.

Yager, R.E. 1991. The constructivist learning model: Towards real reform in science education. *The Science Teacher* 58(6): 52-57.

Constructing *Knowledge* in the Lecture Hall

A Quiz-Based, Group-Learning Approach to Introductory Biology

Daniel J. Klionsky

The standard lecture/note-taking format is not an effective way for students to learn introductory biology. However, it is difficult to implement an active-learning approach unless the students prepare adequately for class. This article describes a format for teaching a large introductory biology course that encourages student preparation prior to class and utilizes problem solving instead of lecturing.

I f I were not aware of it from my own experiences, even a cursory reading of pedagogical literature would reveal that there are inherent flaws in the lecture/note-taking teaching format. As many have noted, this approach leads to passive learning that results in poor retention of information and does not encourage the flexibility, inquiry skills, or higher-order

Daniel Klionsky is a professor, department of molecular, cellular, and developmental biology and of biological chemistry, University of Michigan, 830 North University, Ann Arbor, MI 48109-1048; e-mail: klionsky@umich.edu.

thinking that are necessary for handling the increasing scientific knowledge base (Ahern-Rindell 1999; Crowther 1999; Lord 1994). Yet, as concisely stated by Lord (1994), "the present way we teach our discipline to undergraduates simply does not stimulate active learning." Accordingly, numerous articles suggest methods for shifting the focus from teaching to learning (Caprio et al. 1998; Fortner 1999; Herman 1999; Hufford 1991; Martin 1995).

The concept of active learning suggests that it is incumbent upon the student to take an active role in the learning process. Not all active learning has to take place in the classroom; it can also occur

through preparation and studying. However, most students do not prepare by studying prior to class and furthermore do not review their notes or the text after class, until an exam is imminent (Lord 1994). I describe an approach that encourages active participation by students before, during, and after class. This approach was adapted to meet the constraints of a large university course that does not have a laboratory component, that serves as a prerequisite to upper-division courses, and that is taught to 250 to 350 students in a fixed-seating lecture hall.

My first goal for this course was to devise a method that would alter the study habits of my students. I wanted to find a way to encourage them to read before coming to class and to later review the material that we covered during class. A second goal was to create a learning environment that fostered constructivism. I had experimented with constructivist and group-learning approaches with my course (Klionsky 1998) and became convinced of their value. To provide the students sufficient exposure to, and realize the benefits of, this methodology, I decided to implement a group-learning approach in all of the "lecture" sessions. Because my introductory course is a prerequisite for four upper-division courses, my goal was to strike a balance between inherently slower group learning and coverage of topics that were pertinent to these other courses.

Altering Study Habits

To encourage the students to complete the assigned reading for my class, I wanted to minimize the amount of material they had to read. In general, introductory textbooks are lengthy. In addition, students often complain that the texts are too broad and cover too much information so that they are difficult to study from. These texts are better as references than study guides (Caprio et al. 1997; Musheno and Lawson 1999). As an alternative to the textbook, I made my lecture notes available to my students prior to class. I included the first two days of notes along with the syllabus, handed out on the first day of class. Because of departmental monetary constraints, the students needed to purchase the remaining notes through an on-campus copy service. The notes are condensed relative to the textbook and cover only the information I consider necessary. The textbook served as a supplementary source of information. As a result, the students only had to read six to eight pages per session.

I took two additional steps to assist the students with the reading. First, each topic was preceded by an outline that would help in organizing the material.

Second, the syllabus included guideline questions for the entire course. These were generally five to ten simple questions covering the key points from the reading. For example, on the topic of energetics some questions I suggested the students should be able to answer were, "What is the starting fuel molecule in glycolysis?", "What is the end product of glycolysis?", and "What is the purpose of fermentation?" All of these points were clearly covered in the reading.

To ensure that students would read even this minimal amount of material, on the first day of class I announced that grades for the course would be based entirely on quizzes—there would be no midterms or final exam. Half of the course grade would be based on reading quizzes that focused on material exclusively derived from my notes. These quizzes would be administered prior to any class discussion, so the reading had to be completed by the time the students arrived for class. The remaining half of the grade would be based on concept quizzes. Material for the concept quizzes was based on problems that the students solved in groups.

Problem-Solving Sessions

Class met twice a week for two hours per session. On the first day, I explained the course policies and the rationale behind the problem-solving approach. The students were overjoyed to hear that there were no large exams. This resulted in an immediate and unanticipated reduction in anxiety that was almost palpable. Large one-day exams that typically account for 25 to 50 percent of the course grade put enormous pressure on students and are not especially conducive to effective learning. I also pointed out that grading would be done on an absolute scale because I wanted to create an atmosphere that fostered interactions and reduced any sense of competition (Kohn 1992; Malacinski and Zell 1995).

Finally, I made the point that the

students would work in groups and that answers would reflect the group's consensus. In this way, I hoped to make the students more willing to share their responses. Furthermore, by soliciting responses from the entire class I avoided putting pressure on individual students or groups to answer questions. As an additional benefit, by seeing how many groups responded correctly to questions, I had an easy way of measuring the class' comprehension on each topic, a more effective approach than simply asking for questions from individuals.

The second day of class started with the first reading quiz. I had to ensure that these quizzes were relatively simple and straightforward. The reading quizzes were only meant to demonstrate that the students had done the reading and answered the guideline questions. In addition, I wanted to provide a positive reinforcement for studying. The reading quizzes were designed to be three or four questions that took approximately five minutes to answer. On the topic of energetics, typical quiz questions based on the guideline questions from the syllabus were, "What is the main useful product of the TCA cycle?" and "Name an end-product of fermentation."

After the quizzes were collected, I lectured for 10 minutes on that day's topics and answered questions. The majority of class time was devoted to problem solving. I thought it was essential that I set the right tone for group learning so that the students could see its value right away and gain confidence in the approach. The first subject we were going to cover was carbohydrate structure and function. I asked each student to list five carbohydrates they routinely encountered. Then I had them exchange the list with a neighbor. This step forced them to interact with another student in a very simple way. Next I asked them to raise their hands if their neighbor's list had at least one item that was different from their own. Almost every hand went up. I then pointed out that

By demanding that students take responsibility for the reading, I could eliminate the need for excessive lecturing. This in turn afforded me the time to demonstrate how to solve problems on a range of material and permitted the class to work on the problems in a group setting.

students would be taking advantage of each other's knowledge and understanding. I followed this exercise with specific examples of carbohydrates in our lives, such as lactose intolerance and the reason some milk has *Lactobacillus acidophilus* for breaking down the lactose into digestible monosaccharides.

Now that the students were warmed up, I put up the first question on the overhead: "If you add glucose to a jar with oil and water and mix the contents, where will the glucose end up?" I told them to form groups of two to four people and to discuss the question for a few minutes. Because the seats are fixed in my lecture hall, the groups tended to be two or three people sitting next to each other. Somewhat to my surprise, the students had no hesitation engaging in discussions with their classmates. I attribute this to the fact that they had done the reading and were prepared to discuss the material.

When I decided that enough time had been permitted for discussion, I asked for group responses. I stressed every time that these were group responses, therefore I would generally say something like, "Raise your hand if your group thinks the answer is that glucose ends up in the water phase. Raise your hand if your group thinks it ends up in the oil phase," etc. After getting the responses from the class, I would go over the answers.

Each subsequent day started with a concept quiz based on the material from the previous problem-solving session. Initially, I administered the concept quiz at the end of the class session immediately following the in-class problem solving. However, several problems occurred with this approach. With the second quiz at the end of the class, it was almost impossible to get the students to continue working after the quiz was over. That is, in the minds of the students, taking a quiz signalled the end of class no matter what time it was. In addition, students would tend to leave as soon as they finished the quiz, which was disruptive for those completing their quizzes and made collecting quizzes difficult. In contrast, with both quizzes at the start of class, I could continue with problem solving until the very end of the session. Accordingly, the conceptual quiz was

moved to the following day and at the start of each class I administered the concept quiz from the last session's topic.

The problems on the concept quizzes were substantially more difficult than those on the reading quizzes. For example, on the topic of energetics a typical question was, "Describe what happens to your muscle cells if you exercise strenuously and run out of oxygen." Administering this quiz in the following class session allowed students time to study the material and seek help from classmates, the instructor, and/or the teaching assistants. I think this modification also helped with longer term retention because the students were encouraged to review their notes prior to taking the quiz. Following the concept quiz, I gave the students a couple of minutes to look at their notes and then administered the reading quiz for that day's topics. The remaining class time was spent with problem solv-

ing preceded by a few minutes of lecture to highlight important points from the reading. This format was followed throughout the course.

Assessment

Two methods were used to assess the value of the modified learning format. First, I monitored scores on quizzes in cases where I purposely used the exact same question as in previous years when I had taught using a lecture format. As seen in figure 1, the students generally performed better when they had learned the material through the quiz-based approach. There were exceptions to this trend, in particular with material on the topics of DNA replication and transcription as discussed below. It is also important to note that this method of evaluation may be biased. I placed a much greater emphasis on problem solving when using the quiz-based, group-learning format. Accordingly, it is not surprising to see that

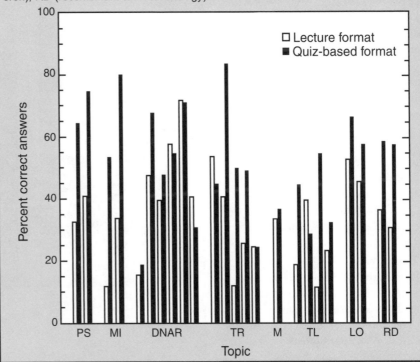

Figure 1. *Comparision of scores using the lecture format and the quiz-based format.*

Scores on identical problems from midterms administered during lecture-based teaching and from quizzes administered during quiz-based learning formats. The results are presented in pairs where each pair of bars represents the percent of correct answers on a single question from a class where teaching/learning took place through the indicated format. The represented topics are: PS (photosynthesis); MI (mitosis and meiosis); DNAR (DNA replication); TR (transcription); M (mutation); TL (translation); LO (lac operon); RD (recombinant DNA technology).

the students generally performed better on exam questions when they learned the material through this approach.

Second, student evaluation of the instructor and course using the quiz-based method were compared to those from the same instructor and course using a lecture format. Students were asked to rate separately both the instructor and course on a five-point scale ranging from "excellent" to "poor." Figure 2 shows evaluations for the course that I taught through a standard lecture format at the same time of the year (fall 1996) to control for seasonal differences in student performance, a course taught in the same year (spring 1999) to control for improvements in my own teaching skills, and a cumulative response from the course taught seven times from 1992 to spring 1999 based on 1,491 student responses. A comparison is shown when 225 students learned the material through the quiz-based approach in the fall of 1999.

Two differences are worth noting from these evaluations. First, the students rated both the instructor and course higher when they learned the material through problem solving. In fact, I received the highest evaluations I have ever gotten in nine years of teaching this course. Second, under the lecture format, the students consistently gave the instructor the highest percentage of scores in the "excellent" category while the course material ranked predominantly in the "very good" range. In contrast, when using the quiz-based approach the course now also received a majority of scores in the "excellent" range. That is, student appreciation for the course itself improved substantially relative to when the course was offered in the lecture format. Written student evaluations indicated that the students found the numerous quizzes challenging but beneficial and included comments such as the following:

- "The quizzes were so much more helpful in learning the material because we were forced to keep up in class and really understand the material."
- "The quizzes . . . allowed us to see our improvement in the class or where we needed to review."

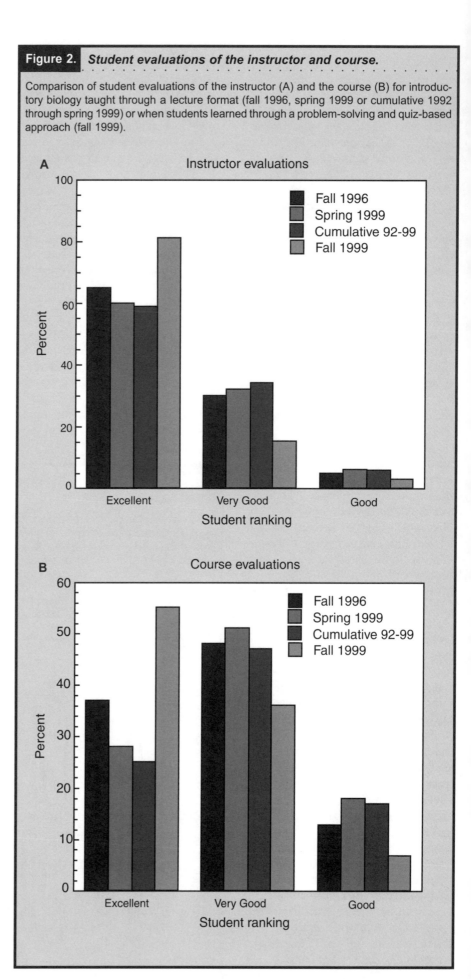

Figure 2. *Student evaluations of the instructor and course.*

Comparison of student evaluations of the instructor (A) and the course (B) for introductory biology taught through a lecture format (fall 1996, spring 1999 or cumulative 1992 through spring 1999) or when students learned through a problem-solving and quiz-based approach (fall 1999).

Photos courtesy of the author

The author has used the group problem-solving approach in a large class with fixed seats and in a smaller class with moveable chairs, as shown in the photo.

- "Learning material ahead of lecture really helped . . ."
- "Quizzes made me learn the material beforehand and review it after, so I learned the material three times, instead of only once."

Approach Concerns

Motivation: It is clear that my approach advocates the use of a large number of quizzes. I am aware that there is some controversy concerning the use of grading as an extrinsic motivator (Kohn 1991). However, based on my own experience I have to agree with Slavin (1991) that when students are not self-motivated, an extrinsic reward may be helpful. The students in my class have many demands on their time, real or perceived. Few are sufficiently motivated to prepare adequately for this required course. Students have told me, however, that without the reading quizzes they simply would not read prior to class. They make a cost-benefit analysis and prepare for other classes that demand their immediate attention.

Part of my justification for using frequent quizzes is that I think the positive reinforcement is likely to make students more active learners. If students are prepared, they will have a greater sense of success in the course and are more likely to participate. This encourages a cycle of preparation and active involvement. Conversely, if I do not force them to prepare, I condone a cycle marked by a lack of understanding and a feeling of futility that only serves to distance these students further from the subject. Finally, most of my students have not experienced active-learning approaches. In general, students who are accustomed to a standard lecture/note-taking format are uncomfortable with the idea of eliminating lectures (Caprio et al. 1998; Orzechowski 1995). The quiz format provides a level of familiarity that eases this transition.

Time: Handing out and collecting two quizzes per day took approximately 25-30 minutes per two-hour session even though each quiz was designed to take five to seven minutes to complete. While this may seem like a large amount of time, it was well worth it. First, there are the benefits of frequent quizzes discussed below. Second, because I could rely on the students being prepared and could hold them accountable for the material, I did not need to lecture at length. This more than compensated for the time lost in administering quizzes. In addition, the time I did have available was spent in more productive ways, such as problem solving.

Balance: I ended up lecturing to my students approximately 20 percent of total class time. Some topics, however, lend themselves extremely well to problem solving and group discussion and others do not. For example, cellular energetics and the *lac* operon (Klionsky 1998) seem particularly well suited for problem solving. I have also found a way to cover organelle structure and function through group learning (Klionsky and Tomashek 1999). I thought this approach was less successful with DNA replication, transcription, and translation. I think these subjects were sufficiently difficult that the students did not gain a good understanding simply from reading the notes. In hindsight, the students would have done better with these topics had I devoted more time to lecturing and had them do fewer problems. Striking a balance between lecturing and group work is key to a successful approach (Airasian and Walsh 1997).

Reading: Most of the students appreciated the brevity of my notes. Some students indicated, however, that they could not understand a topic because it was not explained thoroughly enough in the notes. There is clearly a trade-off between detailed and concise reading assignments. At the start of the course, I probably overemphasized the need to read the notes that I provided instead of the textbook. It would have helped if I pointed out the availability of the assigned text whenever questions came up in the reading or when we were covering more difficult topics. Alternatively, modifications to my notes including expansion of some areas could eliminate this problem.

Grading: I was able to have graduate teaching assistants and undergraduate readers grade the quizzes. Clearly, grading this number of quizzes in a large class is very time consuming. Without the benefit of student assistance I would have been forced to reduce the total number of quizzes, reduce quiz length, rely more on multiple-choice questions, and/or use midterms instead of the concept quizzes.

Approach Benefits

Keeping up: Many students came to me during office hours to tell me that the quizzes on the reading forced them to keep up. Furthermore, they admitted that they normally do not keep up but felt much better about this class because they actually knew what we were talking about. They even speculated as to how they might benefit from this same approach in their other classes.

Larger participation: Because I required everyone to read before coming to class, a greater proportion of students was able and willing to answer questions. This has the advantage of showing students that they do know the material and that it can be enjoyable to participate, thus encouraging further participation.

Learning style: Some students learn better in groups, while others prefer to think about the material on their own before group discussion. By emphasizing both studying outside of class and in-class problem solving, this approach provides learning opportunities for both types of students.

Feedback: The frequent quizzes gave daily feedback to the students on how well they were learning. This stands in sharp contrast to midterms and especially to a final exam. In general, midterms and final exams do not serve the purpose of being learning aids, but rather they are used solely for assessing what a student has already learned. I was able to see the trend in student responses from the quizzes by visually scanning them before they were even graded. This allowed me to alter my plans for the next day's material prior to the next session. The ability to tailor the coverage of the material to the level of the class that rapidly was a fantastic aid for me and allowed me to move at a pace that fit with the students' needs.

Student and instructor enjoyment: The group-learning approach was fun for me as an instructor. However, that meant getting five to ten questions from students in a lecture hour. When I asked the class to answer a question that I posed, I seldom got more than one or two responses. There was quite a difference in my sense of how well the class was learning the material when I got 50, 100, or even 200 responses per question. Knowing that the class was clearly following the material proved exhilarating. The use of reading quizzes and increased student preparation also meant that a larger proportion of the class asked challenging questions about the material. My role as the instructor was no longer to convey an existing body of knowledge. As a result, class discussions were more likely to head in unplanned directions. I encouraged this type of creative thinking, but I also had to be prepared to respond to unexpected lines of thought.

A Viable Alternative

The approach I have described can be used in large lecture classes, so size is not a limitation. It can also be done without relying on computer-based teaching aids, therefore it is extremely low cost. The use of reading quizzes broke the cycle of lack of student preparation and participation. The large number of quizzes provided frequent feedback to the students and instructor so that we could each gauge learning progress easily.

By demanding that students take responsibility for the reading, I could eliminate the need for excessive lecturing. This in turn afforded me the time to demonstrate how to solve problems on a range of material and permitted the class to work on the problems in a group setting. The use of group learning can improve communication skills and foster self-evaluation of comprehension (Malacinski and Zell 1995). Allowing the students to construct the knowledge to answer the questions I posed should substantially improve their ability to learn the material covered in introductory biology.

Acknowledgments
The author would like to thank Dr. Kenneth Verosub, professor of geology at UC Davis, for his helpful discussions on implementation of in-class group learning, Mark Punzal for assistance during class, David Bay for technical assistance, Drs. Ann Hefner-Gravink and Maria Hutchins for their help with the discussion sections, Lisa Klionsky for editorial assistance, and UC Davis students for their willingness to participate in this experimental approach.

References

Ahern-Rindell, A.J. 1999. Applying inquiry-based and cooperative group learning strategies to promote critical thinking. *Journal of College Science Teaching* 28(3): 203-207.

Airasian, P.W., and M.E. Walsh. 1997. Constructivist cautions. *Phi Delta Kappan* 78(6): 449.

Caprio, M.W., N. Dubowsky, L.B. Micikas, and Y.-Y.J. Wu. 1997. It happened in Phoenix. *Journal of College Science Teaching* 26(5): 319-324.

Caprio, M.W., P. Powers, J.D. Kent, S. Harriman, C. Snelling, P. Harris, and M. Guy. 1998. A path toward inte-grated science—The first steps. *Journal of College Science Teaching* 27(6): 430-434.

Crowther, D.T. 1999. Cooperating with constructivism. *Journal of College Science Teaching* 29(1): 17-23.

Fortner, R.W. 1999. Using cooperative learning to introduce undergradutes to professional literature. *Journal of College Science Teaching* 28(4): 261-265.

Herman, C. 1999. Reading the literature in the jargon-intensive field of molecular genetics. *Journal of College Science Teaching* 28(4): 252-253.

Hufford, T.L. 1991. Increasing academic performance in an introductory biology course. *Bioscience* 41(2): 107-108.

Klionsky, D.J. 1998. Application of a cooperative learning approach to introductory biology. *Journal of College Science Teaching* 27(5): 334-338.

Klionsky, D.J., and J.J. Tomashek. 1999. An interactive exercise to learn eukaryotic cell structure & organelle function. *American Biology Teacher* 61(7): 539-542.

Kohn, A. 1991. Group grade grubbing versus cooperative learning. *Educational Leadership* 48(5): 83-87.

Kohn, A. 1992. *No Contest. The Case Against Competition.* New York: Houghton Mifflin Company.

Lord, T.R. 1994. Using constructivism to enhance student learning in college biology. *Journal of College Science Teaching* 23(6): 346-348.

Malacinski, G.M., and P.W. Zell. 1995. Learning molecular biology means more than memorizing the formula for tryptophan. *Journal of College Science Teaching* 25(3): 198-202.

Martin, G.D. 1995. Cooperative learning in chemistry tutorials. *Journal of College Science Teaching* 25(1): 20-23.

Musheno, B.V., and A.E. Lawson. 1999. Effects of learning cycle and traditional text on comprehension of science concepts by students at different reasoning levels. *Journal of Research in Science Teaching* 36(1): 23-37.

Orzechowski, R.F. 1995. Factors to consider before introducing active learning into a large, lecture-based course. *Journal of College Science Teaching* 24(5): 347-349.

Active Learning in the Lecture Hall

A Nonlaboratory Science Course for the Nonscience Major

Elaine J. Anderson

I was handed *First Steps To Excellence in College Teaching* (1990) by Glenn Ross Johnson during the new faculty orientation at Shippensburg University in August 1994. As I glanced through the 80-page book, I was drawn to the chapters "Enhancing the Lecture" and "Increasing Student Involvement: Discussions, Cooperative Learning, Field Studies, Critical Thinking and Questions All Encourage Student Participation."

After considering these titles, I wondered how instructors could involve students in active learning who meet in large lecture halls. I am sure that I am not the only faculty member struggling with this challenge in light of the pressure to modify the standard lecture approach to teaching.

TRYING SOMETHING NEW

Problems of the Environment is a three-credit, primarily lecture, general education course for nonscience majors at Shippensburg University. Its objective is to increase the knowledge

Elaine J. Anderson is an assistant professor of biology at the Franklin Science Center, Shippensburg University, Shippensburg, PA 17257.

base of students, heighten their global awareness of environmental problems and solutions, and educate them about their responsibilities as informed citizens. The course is generally popular and the sections fill up quickly.

As an instructor of this course, I wanted to involve the students in their own learning experiences. I began by modifying the course requirements and engaging the students in a variety of learning activities.

On the first day of class, I had my students work in small groups on a concept mapping activity. The theory behind using concept maps as an advance organizer to enhance cognition and retention is an outgrowth of Ausubelian cognitive educational psychology (Ausubel). The concept maps employed in my class are drawn from an accompanying workbook (Miller) and are prepared for student use.

I provided additional active learning experiences for the students taking my course in the spring semester of 1995. Each activity was intended to facilitate both content-specific and integrative understanding of the concepts being studied. Essays, special team presentations, a garden project, drawings, and concept mapping challenged the students to apply their knowledge in a

meaningful way (**figure 1**). By incorporating many types of educational experiences into my classroom, assessment of student knowledge was based on performance as well as paper and pencil tests (Marzano).

The students discovered that the textbook was an important resource. They found themselves using their textbooks to seek out information on selected issues, to think about their position on those issues, and to propose solutions. In addition to these tasks, the classes took three 75-point exams, a final 25-point test, and had the opportunity to complete a five-point extra credit project. I also planned supplementary word banks, short lectures, and videos for portions of each class meeting. At the end of each class, I gave an exit quiz for two reasons: to check attendance and to review key concepts. Given the amount of student involvement in their own learning, and the workload this approach demanded of the students, I was curious to read the student evaluations of this course.

STUDENT EVALUATION OF THE COURSE

The comments about the course were very positive. Students appreciated the variety of challenges, the pace of the course, the responsibility they had for the various projects, and the opportunity to do well, if not on the tests then on the many projects. They were convinced that they had learned more than they had intended, and had become far more sensitive to environmental problems. Planting the perennial garden for Earth Week was a high point for the class because it added a "lab" component to an otherwise classroom course. The few negative remarks related to the amount of work they had to complete, the difficulty in attaining points needed for an A (achieved by the most industrious students), and the frustration that comes with being and acting environmentally conscious.

As for my opinion of the course's outcome, I believe that the assessment and evaluation of each student's performance was comprehensive. Feedback to students took place as quickly as possible. I clearly stated the grading criteria and point values for each task up front. However, an assignment rubric might have enhanced the students' outcome on the tasks. I also found I had to modify the original 12 essay assignment to six essays due to the overwhelming time demand to correct papers. Even so, the overall grade distribution for the combined classes was skewed to the left: 39.1 percent were A's; 49.05 percent B's; 5.95 percent C's; 2.45 percent D's; 1.15 percent F's; and 1.15 percent were withdrawals.

I would recommend that faculty attempting the above-described assignments use a computerized "gradebook," "micrograde," or other software due to the large number of grades being entered per student. Having a lab assistant or clerk to enter grades would indeed be a bonus.

My reward came in the form of a student comment that made it all seem worthwhile: "I am going to recommend you to teach an honors course. This was great!"

DISCUSSION

I believe that this teaching approach was successful because I involved the class from the start, with concept mapping as an advance organizer (Ausubel), and in collaboration on the concept map as their first active learning task. The skills for cooperative learning were developed slowly, beginning with small challenges and growing into much larger ones. In fact, classroom learning pace was a topic discussed in a recent article by Orzechowski (1995). He states "Don't try too much in the beginning, especially with students who lack prior experience and skills in group learning" and "Don't surprise the class midway through a course with a drastic departure from what they are expecting from you." I spread active learning experiences throughout the semester at a steady rate. Students became more and more skilled in working together, and their ability to team up successfully on concept mapping activities improved with practice (Cliburn).

Generally, a course designed to elicit active learning takes time to design, is evaluation intensive, and is challenging for all involved—faculty and students alike. It demands good resources, an excellent textbook intended to stimulate the reader, as is done in Miller's (1995) text, and significant energy on the part of the faculty leading the class. ❑

References

Arnaudin, Mary W., Joel J. Mintzes, Carolyn S. Dunn, and Thomas S. Shafer. 1984. Concept mapping in college science teaching. *Journal of College Science Teaching* 14(2): 117-21.

Ausubel, David P. 1963. *The Psychology of Meaningful Learning*. New York: Grune and Stratton.

Cliburn, Joseph W. Jr. 1990. Concept maps to promote meaningful learning. *Journal of College Science Teaching* 19(4): 212-217.

Johnson, Glenn Ross. 1990. *First Steps To Excellence In College Teaching*. Madison, WI: Magna Publications, Inc.

Marzano, Robert, Debra Pickering, and Jay McTighe. 1993. *Assessing Student Outcomes; Performance Assessment Using the Dimensions of Learning*. VA: Association of Supervision and Curriculum Development.

Moreira, Marco A. 1979. Concept maps as a tool for teaching. *Journal of College Science Teaching* 8(6): 283-86.

Miller, Jr., and G. Tyler. 1995. *Environmental Science: Working with the Earth*. 5th ed. Belmont, CA: Wadsworth Publishing Company.

Orzechowski, Raymond F. 1995. Factors to consider before introducing active learning into a large, lecture-based course. *Journal of College Science Teaching* 24(5): 347-349.

Figure 1. Problems of the Environment Active Learning Experiences.

Concept Mapping: *I gave a small group (3-4) of students the concept pieces in an envelope and asked them to assemble the pieces into a logical map of interrelated issues, then discuss and explain their map. The first experience is designed with a self check.*

Environmental House: *Students worked alone or in groups of two or three to design an environmentally friendly house. This exercise demanded environmental awareness and challenged students to recall factual information for use in the design. Each student or group presented the house drawing to the class with an explanation of the design and biome the house was intended for.*

Field Project: *In honor of Earth Week, the class planted a perennial garden in front of the science building. Each student in the class selected the group he/she wanted to be part of for the planting experience. On planting day, everyone participated in one of the groups: starters, bushes, bulbs, plants, or finishers. The university paper covered the project and published a picture of the class planting the garden.*

Unit of Study
Special Teams: *The students were divided into five groups. I gave each group a topic and three tasks to divide among themselves. Their assignment was to prepare a presentation for the class on a given date. The tasks included discussing issues, solutions, and answering 10 test questions.*

Critical Thinking: *Each student was asked to write six essays on assigned environmental issues. I asked that the student take a firm position and defend it.*

The Lecture Facilitator:
Sorcerer's Apprentice

Supporting Students *and* Teachers in the Large Lecture

Large lecture courses pose unique problems to instructors. One way to avoid the problems of high enrollment and minimal student-instructor interaction is to use lecture facilitators. Not only can facilitators help with group work, operate the classroom technology, and perform demonstrations, facilitators can put into practice inquiry-based techniques essential for their future careers as science faculty.

Donald P. French and
Connie P. Russell

nquiry-based, problem-based, and other active-learning strategies are advocated as means to enhance students' lecture experiences (e.g., Brewer and Ebert-May 1997; Lord 1998; Siebert and McIntosh 2001). But despite the benefits, instructors are often reluctant to employ modern teaching practices because of budgetary or space constraints that have forced even larger class sizes, making involvement with students during problem-solving sessions or collaborative exercises difficult.

Multimedia-supplemented learning, another strategy, may help students visualize processes better (Sanger and Greenbow 1997), but computer technology often ties instructors to the equipment and compels them to split their attention between thinking about the

technology and interacting with students. Also for some faculty, a desire to incorporate multimedia in the classroom is tempered by their apprehension about using the equipment. To whom can faculty turn for help in this era of limited university resources and overwhelming teacher demands? Is this the opportunity to shape future faculty?

Our solution was to add lecture facilitators to our lecture sections. Although having graduate or undergraduate assistants in the lecture is not a new idea, their role in inquiry-oriented courses such as ours is different. Our lecture facilitators act as "guides" by interacting with student groups, presenting multimedia materials, performing demonstrations, and producing graphical organizers.

Course Structure

In the fall of 1998, the life sciences departments at Oklahoma State University consolidated three introductory biology courses into one mixed-majors, general education, biology course consisting of six lecture sections with enrollments between 126 and 189 students in each. The traditional, expository format of the original courses was replaced with one that incorporates various techniques designed to engage students in constructing concepts. Facilitators play a key role in assisting in the lecture sections of this student-centered course.

Each one- to two-week segment of the course is organized around a particular "scenario" in which the class applies one or more concepts to solve a problem or explain a phenomenon. We designed the scenarios to establish a context for learning and so we could integrate different concepts or information (e.g., natural selection, secondary metabolites, cellular respiration) at dif-

Donald French is an associate professor, department of zoology, Oklahoma State University, 430 LSW, Stillwater, OK 74078; e-mail: dfrench@okstate.edu. Connie Russell is an assistant professor, department of biology, Angelo State University, San Angelo, TX 76909; e-mail: Connie.Russell@angelo.edu.

ferent levels of organization (e.g., ATP production, thermogenesis in animals and plants, energy pyramids).

We open each scenario with a multimedia presentation that typically tells a story, e.g., a trip to the rainforest to watch indigenous people capture fish using extract from plants, a plane crash on the Galapagos Islands, or a visit to the desert and the tundra. The presentations incorporate questions (e.g., "What is causing the fish to gasp at the surface?" or "What accounts for the rapid spread of a form of tuberculosis among these people that is rarely seen elsewhere?") that the students answer in the form of a hypothesis. The students work in groups to prepare written suggestions that they share in a class discussion. Alternatively, after holding brainstorming sessions, the suggestions are written on an electronic whiteboard for all to see and discuss. The lessons then proceed to mini-lectures, demonstrations, and group problem-solving sessions, all while using multimedia materials and live demonstrations to guide the students. The multimedia materials create a framework for discussion.

Because the interconnections among various concepts and processes are not always obvious to students, we illustrate relationships using concept maps and flow charts. These may be drawn before, during, or after class in either free hand or with the electronic whiteboard (to display and record strokes) or *Inspiration©* (Inspiration Software, Inc.) (for handouts, web pages, or multimedia presentations).

Helping 41-63 groups of students during group work periods, operating the classroom technology, performing demonstrations, managing class materials, and producing concept maps was more than we imagined a single faculty member could do. We needed a second

SCI LINKS®
THE WORLD'S A CLICK AWAY

Keyphrase: Instructional Strategies
Go to: http://www.scilinks.org
Enter code: JCST117

instructor in each lecture and created the lecture facilitator to fill that niche.

Finding Facilitators

The life sciences departments could not afford to hire the minimum of six additional teaching assistants to staff the lecture sections of the introductory course with facilitators. Therefore, we revamped a graduate-level, three-credit course, Teaching Zoology, into a course for facilitators. The lecture facilitators taking Teaching Zoology assist the instructors in the above-described course, becoming, in effect, the second instructors.

Enrollment in Teaching Zoology is by permission only. We recruit graduate students or seniors who possess a strong interest in teaching science or science education at the college or high school level. Facilitators attend all meetings of one lecture section and a one-hour seminar each week. In the first few meetings, the facilitators become familiar with the software and curriculum to be used and discuss any problems or issues they may encounter. Subsequent seminar meetings focus on the philosophy and pedagogy involved in inquiry-based teaching and related topics selected by students. The required text for the course is *Methods of Effective Teaching and Course Management* (Siebert et al. 1997), which we supplement with readings that the instructor or students select from current primary literature.

Facilitators were matched to lecture sections based on their schedules and the personality of the lecture instructor. We made an effort to put together instructor-facilitator teams that could both establish a good working relationship and compensate for each other's strengths and weaknesses.

A Facilitator's Typical Day

A normal day for a facilitator begins with a meeting with the course instructor to discuss and plan classroom instruction for the scenario. All instructors and facilitators have copies of a standard set of notes created by the faculty members who developed the course. They also use a standard set of multimedia presentations which the authors, and several undergraduate assis-

---

Figure 1. *Example of the software lecture facilitators use to lead lessons.*

The button bar at the bottom of the screen and the drop down menu [Navigation Hyperlinks] available from the menu bar at the top allow facilitators to navigate to different parts of the lesson at the instructor's discretion. The facilitators can display terms from a scenario-specific glossary [Concepts] and a concept map [Concept Map] that provide an overview of the scenario. The facilitators can time group exercises [timer] or display text references [P]. By pointing to "hot spots" on the screen, the facilitator reveals labels or triggers animations when requested.

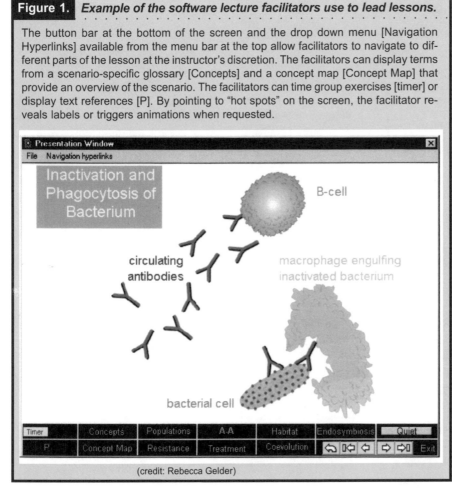

(credit: Rebecca Gelder)

Photos courtesy of the authors

tants programmed using *Authorware©* (Macromedia, Inc.). We created button bars (fig. 1) or drop down menus to allow direct navigation to different points within the lesson. The instructor and facilitator agree on where to start the software on a particular day and which paths they might follow. They also discuss which demonstrations to perform, which questions will be longer group exercises, where the day's lesson might end, what points might be emphasized in concept maps, and any specific instructions on time allotted for in-class activities.

Before each class starts, while the instructor interacts with students or prepares for instruction, the lecture facilitator starts the computer, adjusts room lighting, starts the projector, opens the scenario software to the page previously

designated by the instructor, opens a window to the course webpage to show students any new information (e.g., a tutorial, a concept map, or sample test questions), opens the electronic whiteboard program, opens the concept map produced during the previous lecture, returns quizzes from the previous lecture, and fields student questions.

Typically, the instructor will do a short warm-up to instruction, which may include course announcements. Next, the instructor may have the facilitator conduct a short (about five minutes) review of the previous lecture. During this review the facilitator may use a concept map created during the previous lecture to indicate what he or she considered important points—making connections to concepts both within a scenario and among scenarios. For example, using a concept map that focuses on photosynthesis and its relationship to cellular respiration, the facilitator might ask students, "Where have we used concentration gradients to provide energy before?" or "What similarities did you see between the thylakoid membrane and the inner membrane of a mitochondrion? " (fig. 2).

Next, as the instructor continues with the class, the facilitator would return to the multimedia podium and run the scenario software, watching the instructor for prompts to continue, while simultaneously constructing graphic organizers (concept maps, flow charts), outlines, or lists of terms and concepts for the students. These are drawn on an electronic whiteboard, a marker board connected to the computer, and projected during class or stored for review later. The facilitator operates the multimedia podium throughout the class. From it, the facilitator manages the computers, VCR, videodisc player, visualizer, room lighting, room audiosystem, electronic whiteboard, and the data/video projector.

During each class period there is at least one opportunity for students to answer questions in groups. During these group exercises, the facilitator will distribute answer sheets and answer questions from the students. If no one requests assistance, the instructor and facilitator try to interact with as many groups as possible, particularly those that don't appear to be talking or appear to be struggling. After the exercise, while the instructor contin-

Figure 2. *A concept map drawn by a facilitator during a session on photosynthesis.*

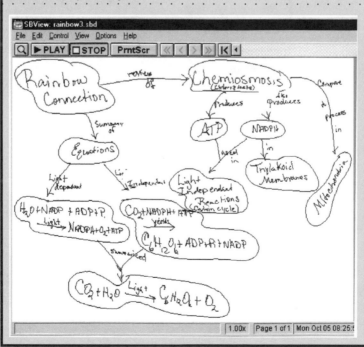

ues with the class, the facilitator collects papers before returning to the computer.

In several scenarios there are in-class demonstrations. For example, we present a demonstration of the effect of temperature on ectotherm activity. The facilitator places a petri dish containing isopods on the visualizer (video camera and light table), adjusts the lighting, zoom, and focus, and projects the image for the whole class to see. The facilitator or the instructor asks the students to predict what will happen if the isopods are placed on an ice-pack and to suggest a hypothesis. After a discussion and perhaps a written assignment, the facilitator places the isopods on an ice pack and the class continues. Because the projector must be switched to project the computer display, the facilitator watches the demonstration and periodically projects the demonstration as the isopods' activity changes. Meanwhile, the instructor and the class can continue to interact. Because many students think the isopods die from the cold, the facilitator then reverses the conditions and repeats the experiment. Without the facilitator, the class flow is easily interrupted by the frequent need to check the experiment.

Facilitators also keep up with the time and remind the instructor (if asked) of time constraints. There are tools built into the software so that facilitators can provide a gentle (and unobtrusive) reminder that time is growing short. At the discretion of the instructor, a facilitator may occasionally instruct the class and the instructor may facilitate.

At the end of the class period the facilitator shuts down the multimedia equipment and gathers up materials brought to class, allowing the instructor to interact with students. It is also important for the facilitators to be available for student questions. Some students are more comfortable asking someone they consider to be a near peer for help and will not hesitate to ask the facilitator during, after, or outside of class rather than "bothering" the instructor.

Survey Responses

We assessed the role of the facilitators using surveys distributed at the middle and end of the semesters. The mid-semester surveys were composed of open-ended

Table 1. *Percentages of students selecting each answer on an end of the semester survey in response to questions about the facilitators.*

	Strongly Agree	Agree	Neither Agree nor Disagree	Disagree	Strongly Disagree
"I liked having the lecture facilitator help with class." (N = 589)					
Section 1	35	37.5	16.7	6.7	4.2
Section 2	11.6	26.8	33.9	15.2	12.5
Section 3	24.7	47.3	21.5	2.2	4.3
Section 4	23.3	50	24.4	2.2	0
Section 5	17.7	47.9	26	5.2	3.1
Section 6	19.2	41	30.8	6.4	2.6
Overall	22.2	41.1	25.3	6.6	4.8
"I liked having the lecture facilitator to help run the computer." (N = 590)					
Section 1	33.6	49.6	14.3	0	2.5
Section 2	13.3	42.5	26.5	8	9.7
Section 3	32.3	46.2	18.3	1.1	2.2
Section 4	29.7	53.8	14.3	1.1	1.1
Section 5	22.9	43.8	27.1	3.1	3.1
Section 6	17.9	50	26.9	3.8	1.3
Overall	25.1	47.5	21	2.9	3.6
"I liked having the lecture facilitator to help with group discussions." (N = 588)					
Section 1	30.3	45.4	17.6	4.2	2.5
Section 2	8.9	22.3	33	22.3	13.4
Section 3	25.8	41.9	28	3.2	1.1
Section 4	24.4	45.6	24.4	5.6	0
Section 5	15.6	40.6	34.4	5.2	4.2
Section 6	12.8	41	33.3	9	3.8
Overall	19.9	39.1	28.1	8.5	4.4

questions (e.g., "What do you think of the idea of having a facilitator in the classroom?" "What do think of the job your lecture facilitator is doing at fulfilling his/her duties"?) presented after a brief description of the facilitators' responsibilities. On the survey given at the end of the spring 1999 semester, students answered the questions presented in table 1 on a five-point Likert-type scale. A Chi-square goodness-of-fit test indicated that students thought favorably of the facilitators' roles in helping with the class ($\chi^2=261.8$, df = 4, p<.0001), in running the computer ($\chi^2=396.5$, df = 4, p<.0001), and in helping with group discussions ($\chi^2=236.7$, df = 4, p<.0001). Contingency Table Analyses indicated significant differences

among the lecture sections for each question ($\chi^2=72$, df = 20, p<.0001; $\chi^2=57.2$, df = 20, p<.0001; $\chi^2=98$, df =20, p<.0001). One of the sections was very different from the others. When that section was excluded, the percentages of students with favorable responses were 69 percent ("help with class"), 76 percent ("run the computer"), and 65 percent ("help with group discussions").

We also assessed opinions of the students and instructors through interviews. On the final survey form, students were asked to list three aspects of the course they liked and three aspects they would change. In sections in which the facilitator was either less involved or irresponsible (as indicated by attendance and instructor's observations), student comments were critical of either the instructor's failure to make use of the facilitator ("all she does is pass out papers") or critical of the performance of the facilitator ("needs to get her act together"). However, in sections in which the facilitators were used to their fullest potential, students readily recognized the value of having that person in the classroom. Many acknowledged that the facilitator freed the instructor to spend more time with them. One student commented that the lecture facilitator "seems to make it easier for the instructor to maintain contact with students" and another stated that the facilitator "made things move along, because there were two people available for questions." Overall, student comments concerning the facilitators were favorable. In the sections with the facilitator with the most teaching experience and freedom to participate in interactive classroom activities, student satisfaction ranged between 73 and 83 percent.

Helping groups of students during the lecture period was more than a single faculty member could do. We needed a second instructor, so we created the lecture facilitator to fill that niche.

Throughout the semester, we asked the instructors to evaluate the role of the facilitator and the job that theirs did. During the first semester (fall of 1998), the instructors were positive to various degrees. At the end of the second semester (spring of 1999), all the instructors were very positive about the concept. They expressed the opinion that the facilitators made the class much easier to teach. Several considered them essential to our style of teaching.

In the spring and fall 1999 classes, the facilitators in Teaching Zoology wrote philosophy of education/teaching statements at the beginning and end of the course. For half the students who handed in a statement there was little change. However, among the others there were some interesting comments. The constructivist/inquiry-based approach was viewed as harder to implement and more work than facilitators had originally thought it would be. Several felt that despite the additional work,

this experience reinforced their desires to use such methods in their future teaching. One facilitator pointed out that "students are not necessarily going to enjoy the experience of good teaching theory." In subsequent interactions with and observations of this facilitator teaching a laboratory, we noticed the facilitator employing these techniques.

Facilitators mentioned that learning should be fun, one of the design criteria for this course. In the philosophy of teaching statements at the end of semester, the nine fall 1999 facilitators, who were all life sciences majors, cited the need for an instructor to make students into active participants. Facilitators commonly stated that instructors should guide students to an understanding of concepts and that traditional lecturing was not a way to promote active participation. This differs from the statements of many at the beginning of the semester who advocated "presentation of material in an easily understood manner" as their teaching philosophy.

Overall, facilitators believe that they have benefited from the experience and that the concept of the facilitator in the classroom is an excellent one. However, facilitators faced a wide range of experiences in this course. Some of the facilitators felt that although the class was a worthwhile experience, they were largely underutilized in their role as a facilitator. Early in the semester, these facilitators were often relegated to paper handling and other mundane jobs. Over the course of the semester, as the facilitator and instructor began to get a sense of how to best work together, all of the facilitators were increasingly given opportunities to interact with students and to lead a more active role in the classroom. However, several of the facilitators still wanted to have more contact with the class. Several facilitators also expressed an interest in learning to use concept maps more effectively in this course and to apply the technique to other courses.

Facilitators see their role in the classroom as a liaison between students and instructors and find that relationship particularly rewarding. The desire to interact more with students, play a more active role in the classroom, and promote the use of concept maps as useful learning tools have been recurring themes among facilitators.

Everyone Benefits

We believe the use of facilitators in our introductory biology course to be unique, valuable, and well received. By managing the multimedia equipment, facilitators allow instructors to concentrate on their remarks, position themselves among the students, and interact more with students.

Facilitators serve as an alternative instructor. Some students felt more comfortable talking to the facilitator both during and after class. Some students would solicit help from either the instructor or the facilitator; some would specifically request help from the facilitator. It was common to see a line of students by the facilitator as well as the instructor. Such interactions also help improve the class because the facilitator can relate the students' problems and concerns to the instructor.

Facilitators provide a different perspective. At times, they interpret a student's question correctly when the instructor misunderstands. They also occasionally spot an instructor's misstatement. One of us (DPF) accidentally gave contradictory information about ABO blood groups to the class while answering a question, then was puzzled at the confused faces of the students until the facilitator politely stepped in and helped. Facilitators tactfully convey such information to the instructor.

Facilitators benefit from and enjoy the experience. The ratings for the experience were extremely high with students indicating that they learned a lot. Many of the facilitators were already familiar with educational theory, yet were happy to discuss it and appreciated the opportunity to try and apply it. It is interesting, and perhaps disconcerting, to note that only one of the facilitators was a doctoral student in the life sciences, a group that Teaching Zoology was intended to target. We believe that if reform in postsecondary science education is to take place, then we must influence graduate students. The experience that graduate students have teaching affects their future teaching style (Druger 1997; Freezel and Myers 1997; Rushin et al. 1997; Myers 1998). We hope that in time we will be able to change this trend and to influence more future faculty in this style of education. For one of us (CPR), as a new professor, this experience has proven invaluable.

Are there some drawbacks to using facilitators? Certainly. Even when screened, some prove unreliable (habitual absenteeism), and this can affect class evaluations. Instructors and facilitators have to develop a rapport to form a good working relationship. In the highest rated sections this was the case. But this takes time and, as one facilitator stated, "communication is important."

The relationship between each instructor-facilitator pair is important. Several facilitators suggested that if everyone met regularly to discuss teaching methods and pedagogy, instructors would accept facilitators as partners faster. Working with a facilitator takes some getting used to, and not all of the instructors used facilitators to the same degree. Faculty, however, become more confident in the facilitator over time. Instructors let those students in whom they had more faith interact more with the class.

Use of facilitators has made the transition from traditional teaching styles to an inquiry-based style much easier for students and faculty. Moreover, this position provides the facilitators with invaluable experience conducting a large lecture course, learning to work with multimedia, and interacting with groups.

Acknowledgment

The authors would like to thank Dr. Janice French, Ms. Jill McNew, and Ms. Elizabeth Noga for their insightful comments on this manuscript. In addition, Ms. Noga helped with analysis of data.

Note

This project was funded in part from a grant by the National Science Foundation (NSF# 9752402). Opinions expressed are those of the authors and not necessarily those of the foundation.

References

Druger, M. 1997. Preparing the next generation of college science teachers. *Journal of College Science Teaching* 26: 424-427.

Ebert-May, D., C. Brewer, and S. Allred. 1997. Innovation in large lectures–Teaching for active learning. *BioScience* 47(9): 601-607.

Feezel, J.D., and S.A. Myers. 1997. Assessing graduate student teacher communication concerns. *Communication Quarterly* 45(3): 110-124.

Lord, T. 1998. Cooperative learning that really works in biology teaching. *The American Biology Teacher* 60(8): 580-588.

Myers, S.A. 1998. GTAs as organizational newcomers: The association between supportive communication relationships and information seeking. *Western Journal of Communication* 62(1): 54-73.

Rushin, J.W., J. De Saix, A. Lumsden, D.P. Streubel, G. Summers, and C. Bernson. 1997. Graduate teaching assistant training. *The American Biology Teacher* 59(2): 86-90.

Sanger, M.J., and T.J. Greenbow. 1997. Students' misconceptions in electrochemistry: Current flow in electrolyte solution and salt bridge. *Journal of Chemical Education* 74(7): 819-823.

Siebert, E.D., M.W. Caprio, and C.M. Lyda, eds. 1997. *Methods of Effective Teaching and Course Management for University and College Science Teachers*. Dubuque, IA: Kendall/Hunt Publishing Company.

Siebert, E.D., and W.J. McIntosh, eds. 2001. *College Pathways to the Science Education Standards*. Arlington, VA: NSTA Press.

Facilitating the Reading/ Discussion Connection in the Interactive Classroom

"Discovery Questions" Help Create Independent Learners

Beverly C. Pestel

A body of research has accumulated from the work of cognitive psychologists and learning theorists that substantiates the value of interactive teaching. This research validates the constructivist epistemology and focuses on the need for students to be actively involved in the learning process (Baird, Fensham, Gunstone, and White, 1991; Brophy, 1992; Caine and Caine, 1991; Newmann, 1991; Prawat, 1993; Rosenshine and Meister, 1992).

A result of this new understanding of the teaching/learning process is a need for teachers to experiment with alternatives to the traditional lecture. Unfortunately, the existing research cannot prescribe the specific strategies that will result in students taking a more active part in the learning process. Teachers must take the basic research that says students learn more thoroughly and efficiently when they are actively involved and devise their own individual strategies for accomplishing this involvement. I hope that in describing what I do, you will find some truths that will help you develop strategies that will work in your class-

Beverly Pestel is Lumsden-Valrance Visiting Lecturer, department of chemistry, Michigan State University, East Lansing, MI 48824.

> *If students are to achieve the higher level of learning that occurs as a result of interactive classroom strategies and discussions, then teachers must accept the responsibility of helping students develop their ability to extract information from textbooks.*

room. Sharing pedagogical experiences can be an effective means of stimulating the development of new strategies for enhancing student learning.

For the past two years I have used a classroom technique that I call "discovery questions." This technique was designed to accomplish two goals: 1) inject an interactive, discussion framework into the classroom, and 2) focus the students' attention on reading and absorbing information from the textbook.

In the interactive classroom, discuss-

ing ideas that help students reach understanding is the priority. Under these circumstances, time restraints require that students assume responsibility for reading the textbook in advance to obtain the basic information that makes these discussions possible.

In the first quarter of the course I use this technique, the classroom discussions build from the students' laboratory experiences. The content is in-depth coverage of material most students have been exposed to in high school. As a result, reading the textbook for basic information is not an issue for most students during the first quarter. It is only during the second quarter that many students face new material for the first time in the context of a discussion-oriented course. Therefore, it is in the second quarter of this course that I introduce "discovery questions."

The factual information that makes classroom discussions possible is available in the textbook. However, because of the prevalence of lecture as a classroom strategy, many students have never been held accountable nor have they been trained to rely on reading to retrieve information. While it is realistic for teachers to expect students to be able to read the textbook to gain this factual information, the fact is that they are not very good at it. Consequently, if students are to achieve the higher level of learning that occurs as a result of interactive classroom strategies and discussions, then teachers must accept the responsibility of helping students develop their ability to extract information from textbooks.

The "discovery question" teaching strategy requires students to read the text and acquaints them with some of the skills in evaluating written material within a classroom-discussion framework. Each question is structured around a specific and limited reading assignment. Since reading for understanding is a problem for students, I assign reading in small chunks on a class-by-class basis instead of assigning a chapter at a time. The discovery question is fitted to a reading assignment that is usually no more than 53 pages in length. I develop the question as I read the assignment myself, pulling out of the reading those ideas or principles that I want the students to focus on and understand. The question encompasses a broad topic and each statement that accompanies this frame is either a true or false statement. Examples of discovery questions are found in **Table 1**.

Questions like the ones in Table 1 are handed out at the beginning of class. Students are given 10-20 minutes to work in groups to determine whether each statement is true or false and prepare a justification for each answer. Essentially, the discovery question becomes the outline for the day's discussion. During the 10-20 minutes that the groups are working on the question, they are reviewing the reading assignment to find answers and are discussing among themselves the justifications for those answers. This activity forces the students to retrieve from the reading assignment those ideas that comprise the substance of the material and to separate fact from explanation.

Early in the quarter, I hand out 3" x 5" cards to each group, ask them to record their names and their answers (not the explanations), and return the cards to me when they are finished. When all of the cards are in, I randomly pull out a card and ask that per-

---

Table 1. Sample Discovery Questions.

• The thermodynamic function, enthalpy...
  i.   ...requires that new energy terms be measured.
  ii. ...must be a state property.
  iii. ...has an absolute value, H, which can be determined.
  iv. ...is a measure of the change in internal energy of a system if no pressure-volume work is done against a constant external pressure.
  v.   ...can be measured using calorimetry if the reaction is run at constant P_{ext}.

• Consider the result of placing 1.0 g of sodium metal in 50 g of water initially at 298K.

$$2Na(s) + 2H_2O(l) \rightleftharpoons 2NaOH(aq) + H_2(g) + Heat$$

This reaction is carried out under two separate conditions: 1) a large closed container fitted with a movable piston, and 2) a small closed flask.

Which of the following statements are valid?
  i.   If the "system" is the reaction as defined above, the "surroundings" are also the same for both cases.
  ii. Work is done in the first case, but not in the second case.
  ii. The change in the internal energy is the same in both cases.
  iv. The heat flow occurring in the first case is greater than in the second case.
  v.   The system will undergo a temperature change that can be used to calculate the heat flow for the system.

---

son for a justification of the group's answer. This procedure has several benefits: I learn students' names; I encourage group cooperation; I know when the students are ready to answer; I enforce individual accountability because the group does not know which member will be called upon to answer for that group; and I make answering the question less threatening because the student is answering for the group rather than him/herself.

I have used this strategy in classes ranging from 20-60 students with no discernable difference in response. In smaller classes, I am able to monitor group conversations in more detail, but the ability to monitor does not appear to be a significant factor in the success to the strategy. The follow-up, full-class discussion appears to be sufficient to ensure that all students have reached an acceptable level of understanding. Depending on the nature of the content and the type of laboratory experiences during any week, the frequency with which I use these questions can vary. On an average, approximately 50

percent of class time is utilized in this manner, and I have not experienced any need to eliminate content because of time restraints.

Student response to this classroom strategy during the second year I used it was remarkably positive. On student evaluations given at the end of every quarter, I received a number of responses directly related to the use of discovery questions. The nature of the comments demonstrates the value students put on this experience. For instance:

"I've enjoyed this class as much by the challenge to my intellect (and my GPA) as the material itself. I especially appreciate the skill at which Dr. Pestel administers group work." "I feel her teaching strategy is very good. We are forced to think in class but that is good because we have to do that on the test." "I like the group work, it helps to learn from each other and teach each other." "She taught in a way that got everyone involved in the learning." "Dr. Pestel has made us all think. She teaches, she doesn't just tell you how to do something, she makes you tell her why you do what you do. She has a way of making a student think." "Her method of forcing the class into discussion was a great way of getting us involved."

I am convinced that one of the reasons for the students' positive responses to this teaching strategy is the result of the explanations I give for using the technique. Students cannot be expected to understand how a particular teaching strategy may benefit them unless the teacher explains the specific nature of that benefit. On the first day of class, I explain to students that my goal is for them to become more independent learners and creative problem-solvers. For this course, the two most prominent aspects of this goal are: 1) that they become better able to gather information from the text, and 2) that they begin to recognize knowledge as their ability to express the information they have and use it to solve problems.

I explain to students how the classroom strategies are designed to address the development of these problem-solving skills. In the case of the discovery question, the students can review and reevaluate the reading assignment. The group involvement in preparing justifications for answers forces them to evaluate their level of understanding. I remind them of my goals for them and how the teaching strategies address those goals continually throughout the course.

Early in the course, many students agree with me when I suggest that reading is a skill they need to develop more fully. On the other hand, it is only after using the technique for a while that they recognize its value in helping them learn—and then only if I repeatedly ask them to consider that possibility.

I have discovered that the more explicit I am about what I am doing in the classroom and why I am doing it, the more positive the response will be both in the amount of learning that occurs and in student attitude toward the course. During the first year that I used this strategy, I explained it during the first week and then never mentioned my motives or goals again. A comparison of student comments made during the first year this strategy was used with those made the second year illustrates just how critical the continual reminder can be. In addition to a few positive comments, the following remarks were made on the first-year evaluations:

"The class needs more in-class instruction." "I feel that the group concept is wrong for this class. It should not be the responsibility of one person to teach the rest of the group what is going on."

In response to the question: What characteristics of your instructor do you consider to be weaknesses? "The way in which chemistry is taught."

In response to the question: How could this course be improved? "Reduce group work." "Rearrange the group work." "Less emphasis on group work." "Reduce group work." "Better format."

Any change is difficult for students, and this type of teaching/learning change can be especially traumatic. Student responsibility in the learning process is much greater in an interactive classroom than in the traditional lecture classroom. This increased responsibility is scary for many students. Negative responses can be expected for this reason alone. Since some level of fear and/or negative feelings cannot be avoided, everything possible needs to be done to minimize the fear and maximize the students' comfort level. The continual reminders appear to be very beneficial in accomplishing this effect.

Maximizing the effectiveness of any pedagogical innovation is an iterative process. For instance, my challenge for next year is to figure out how to address the comments I received this year:

"The group involvement is a good way since we can correct ourselves by asking someone else in the group. Since she wants us to learn on our own experience, she sometimes lets us believe what we say is true for too long."

"Teacher allows students to continue expanding on wrong answers. Makes it hard for us to figure out the right way to do things. When a student gives a wrong answer, the teacher should tell him that he is off track and to try again."

It is important that students be allowed to express their ideas whether they are right or wrong. However, some of the discussions involving wrong answers evidently are troublesome to some students. Where do I draw the line between allowing students to talk and making sure that the correct ideas are communicated clearly to all students?

There are a number of things I enjoy about experimenting with interactive teaching strategies. Foremost among them are the increased dynamics in the classroom and the increase in the challenge to continually adjust to students' needs and perceptions. The challenges and the risks involved in introducing classroom innovations are very real, but when successful the benefits just can not be beaten. ❑

Acknowledgment
Many of the discovery questions the author uses were developed in collaboration with the following colleagues at Rose-Hulman Institute of Technology: Michael Mueller, Dennis Lewis, and David Erwin.

References
Baird, J.R., P.J. Fensham, R.F. Gunstone, and R.T. White. 1991. The importance of reflection in improving science teaching and learning. *Journal of Research in Science Teaching* 28(2): 163-182.

Brophy, J. 1992. Probing the subtleties of subject-matter teaching. *Educational Leadership* 49(7): 4-8.

Caine, R.N., and G. Caine. 1991. *Making Connections: Teaching and the Human Brain.* Alexandria, Va.: Association for Supervision and Curriculum Development.

Newmann, F.M. 1991. Linking restructuring to authentic student achievement. *Phi Delta Kappan* 72(6): 458-463.

Prawat, R. S. 1993. The value of ideas: Problem versus possibilities in learning. *Educational Researcher* 22(6): 5-16.

Rosenshine, B. and C. Meister. 1992. The use of scaffolds for teaching higher-level cognitive strategies. *Educational Leadership* 49(7): 26-33.

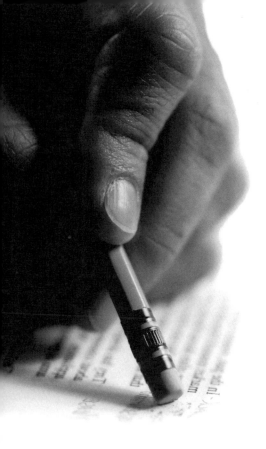

A Peer-Reviewed Research Assignment for Large Classes

Honing Students' Writing Skills in a Collaborative Endeavor

LaRhee Henderson and Charisse Buising

One way science educators can integrate writing, critical-thinking and team-building skills into their curriculum is by incorporating a collaborative, peer-evaluated research paper assignment. This type of exercise reduces an instructor's heavy grading load and, more importantly, teaches students to research scientific literature, synthesize information, and review the work of their peers.

Writing is a very valuable learning tool (Holiday 1994; Jewett and John 1991; Prain 1996; Trombulak 1989). It requires active engagement with the subject matter, representing a form of student-centered learning. Furthermore, writing a research paper for a science course teaches students skills not obtained from a standard series of exams and problem sets. In addition to developing writing skills, students learn to do literature searches, read scientific papers, evaluate material, and build connections between pieces of data and information to construct a larger, more coherent story.

Logistically, however, writing assignments for large classes can pose a problem. Instructors of large science classes typically bear a heavy grading load of homework and exams, not leaving much time for student assistance and grading of substantive writing assignments like research papers. We overcame this problem by developing a writing exercise in which students work in collaborative groups and evaluate papers by their peers, replicating the work of professional scientists.

Collaborative, Peer-Reviewed Papers

As practicing scientists, we routinely write grant proposals, articles, and presentations in collaborative groups. When we approach these collaborative writing tasks, we usually divide them into sections that we later merge into a final product. To make this real-world connection with the research paper project, we have students emulate this process that scientists use.

To begin the process, we divide our large biochemistry class of about 150 students into small groups of three to five students. The groups then select research ideas from a list of 13 topics that we distribute, with two or three groups researching the same topic. Typically based on case studies, topics include molecular aspects of fructose intolerance, hyperlipidemia type I, myocardial infarction, cholera, Ehlers-Danlos syndrome, rheumatoid arthritis, and hypothyroidism.

After choosing a topic, groups then subdivide the assignment among the members. For example, students could divide a report dealing with Parkinson's disease into: (1) dopamine and its role in neurotransmission, (2) current theories on the causes of the disease, (3) current treatments of the disease and their molecular basis, and (4) interviews with local health professionals, friends, or family with personal experiences with the disease.

Returning to their groups, students organize their individual sections into a draft of the research paper. Thus, each student contributes some portion of the paper but the group shares the final product. By mid-semester, groups must complete their drafts and exchange them with another group, preferably one working on the same topic, for peer-group evaluation. Each member of the group completes this evaluation individually. The instructor also evaluates the draft.

Although students have considerable freedom in developing their papers, we distribute grading criteria outlining our performance expectations (figure 1), which both the students and instructors use when evaluating the papers. The criteria are interpreted differently by the peer groups and the instructor, according to experience and position. Thus, the

LaRhee Henderson is an associate professor of chemistry and Charisse Buising is an associate professor of biology, Drake University, Des Moines, IA 50311; e-mail: LaRhee.Henderson@drake.edu and Charisse.Buising@drake.edu.

grading criteria allows for some flexibility but also provides a framework to guide the students as they compose their drafts and evaluate each other.

Students have one week to evaluate each other's drafts and write comments and suggestions. This draft review does not count toward the students' project grade. The groups have two weeks to rewrite their drafts, based on the returned comments, and submit their final reports.

Groups that have worked on the same topic exchange their final reports, evaluating them according to the original criteria grid in figure 1. Since they have each researched the same topic, each group should be considered an authority qualified to evaluate another paper on that particular subject. In the end, each paper has two peer evaluations. Again, the evaluation of the final paper is due within one week.

Electronic Bulletin Board

Students post their final research papers on an electronic bulletin board so they can easily be accessed. Those viewing the papers may post comments and suggestions, which allows the entire class to interact on all the topics and provides the student authors with valuable, unbiased suggestions before their poster presentations. Readers also receive a preview of the breadth of topics examined by the class and the op-

---

Figure 1. *Peer-Group Evaluation Criteria of Research Paper*

Points will be awarded by the criteria described below. Please note that you may assign intermediate amounts of points; the points described are given as a guideline. In your final evaluations please assign grades to fit the following: F: The paper did not meet the minimum requirements. D: The paper met some requirements, but did not meet many of the stated expectations. C: The paper adequately met the criteria. It contained all the required parts. It was clearly presented, well organized and well written. B: The paper met the criteria and added quality by creativity, extra research, or some other enhancement. The authors did a good job of combining resource materials into a clear, cohesive presentation and illustrated their clear grasp of the material. A: The paper met the criteria and exceeded expectations. It shows initiative, creativity, research depth and clear growth of the authors' perceptions as they compiled their work (they went beyond a simple rewriting of resource material).

Criteria	F (0-50%)	D (65%)	C (75%)	B (85%)	A (95%)	Points
Well researched (20 points) Quality references (respected, current journals are included) Shows variety (e.g., journals, texts, personal contacts, etc.) Substantiates the points of the authors						
Well written (30 points) Uses good grammar, is easy to read and understand, is well organized Illustrations enhance the content References are properly cited throughout text Content is not plagiarized (style and vocabulary are consistent with student)						
Science-based (40 points) Scientific problem is clearly described Paper has a molecular focus (at least one molecular aspect studied in depth) Physiological events are established Science is correct (corroborated by appropriate references)						
Other (10 points) Uses creative enhancement (e.g., illustrations, interviews, pictures, testimonials)						
Total Points						
Summary justification of your evaluation:						

---

portunity to read them in depth. In addition, students can leave the papers on the electronic bulletin board for subsequent classes to read as examples of previous works.

Poster Presentations

Once the groups complete their final research papers, those who shared a topic collaborate on another public presentation format: a poster display. This exercise, combined with the small group composition phase, brings a healthy balance of competition and cooperation to the exercise. Students can discuss corrections and improvements to their original compositions to help them determine the final presented product.

The posters are set up in the laboratory and open to the public for two to three days. Student presenters station themselves beside their posters at specified times to answer questions. All students in the class must tour the displays and complete peer-group evaluations of each, using guidelines that we distribute in advance (figure 2). That way the class becomes acquainted with the research topics explored by other teams.

Grading

The students' final grades reflect the following three components: the research paper and the poster (both based on the instructor's scores and peer-group evaluation) and the instructor's score of peer-group evaluation (how well each student evaluated another group's paper).

Peer-Group Evaluation

Often, students are uncomfortable evaluating their peers and will ask us for permission to give lower scores. They are also reluctant to accept criticism from peers and come to us with complaints about their peer evaluators. In general, students hope to receive nearly perfect scores on writing assignments, and when negative judgments come from peers, they find the comments difficult to accept.

For this reason the criteria grid is very useful, taking much of the subjectivity out of the process. It is also

photos courtesy of the authors

Two students at Drake University in Des Moines, IA, discuss their research findings with their industry project mentor, Dr. John Howard.

Figure 2.   *Peer-Group Evaluation Criteria of Poster Presentation*

Please evaluate the other groups' poster presentations according to the following criteria:

1. General Appearance and Style

Criteria: Readable, Orderly, Accessible, Attractive

Point Assignment: Exceeds all criteria through creativity and originality =15 points;

Meets all criteria = 10 points;

Does not meet some of the criteria = 5-8 points.

Comments:

2. Content

Criteria: Abstract: Concisely summarizes the main features of the report. Case Study: Presents the case in a format that allows the reader to quickly identify the problem and its symptoms. Background: Concisely explains the molecular principles related to the problem. Research: Clearly outlines the current thinking on the molecular basis of the problem and the associated symptoms and treatments. Scope and Focus: Basic biochemical concepts are carried through the report to link a disease's cause, symptoms, and treatment. The scope of the paper is appropriate and well defined.

Point Assignment: Exceeds all criteria through creativity and originality = 60-70 points;

Meets most criteria = 50-60 points;

Does not meet some of the criteria = 40-50 points;

Does not meet most of the criteria = 30-40 points.

Comments:

3. Student Presentation

Criteria: Student was professional, enthusiastic, knowledgeable, and able to communicate project and results clearly and effectively.

Point Assignment: Exceeds all criteria through creativity and originality =15 points;

Meets all criteria = 10 points;

Does not meet some of the criteria = 5-8 points.

Comments:

Figure 3. *Intra-Group Evaluation Criteria of Peer Performance*

Please evaluate each individual member of your group in terms of his or her contribution to the class assignments according to the following scale. The individual results of the survey will be kept confidential but summaries of the group evaluations of an individual's contribution will be available to that individual. Your evaluations will be considered in the grading process, so think about your comments carefully and provide specific details to justify your evaluation.

8. *Participated fully* (extended learning for self and others): performed assigned part of the project successfully, took initiatives that helped make significant contributions to the quality of the project; took an active leadership role on the project, helping everyone understand and perform successfully.

7. *Participated fully* (extended learning for self): performed assigned part of the project successfully; took initiatives that helped make significant contributions to the quality of the project.

6. *Participated fully* (understood basic concepts): performed assigned part of the project independently, reliably, and responsibly; made valuable contributions to the project as an individual member of the research team without requiring prompting from the rest of the group.

5. *Participated fully* (lacked some understanding and missed connections): performed assigned part of the project responsibly; made valuable contributions to the project as an individual member of the research team when given the group's guidance.

4. *Participated occasionally* (lacked some understanding and missed connections): performed part of the project; made limited contributions that were primarily guided and directed by the rest of the group.

3. *Participated only when called upon* (not active): performed part of the project, made limited contributions when solicited by the rest of the group.

2. *Participated in structured exercises only:* participated in only the visible portions of the project (oral presentations, poster display, etc.) but did not contribute to the work of the project.

1. *Attended but did not participate:* usually physically present at exercises but not engaged with the project; did not contribute a significant effort to the planning, execution, or delivery of the project.

0. *Did not attend.*

Comments: (Explain your rating for this student)

A student presents his team's work to his peers. The audience then evaluates both the content of the poster and the student's oral presentation.

the reason that we grade the quality of each student's peer-group evaluation; students take the evaluation more seriously when they know that their comments will affect another person's grade and that the thoroughness and validity of those comments will affect their own grades.

Intra-Group Evaluation

We do not specifically dictate the working dynamics within the groups. We do, however, make it clear that we expect each group member to contribute. We do so through instructions to the class as well as through intra-group evaluation of peer performance, conducted periodically throughout the semester. We use an evaluation tool that enumerates performance characteristics that correspond to scores that range from 1 to 8. Students evaluate each member of their own group using the numerical score and by providing written comments (figure 3). The instructors take into account the results of the intragroup evaluation of peer performance when assessing the components of a student's grade.

We keep the individual evaluations confidential, though we provide summaries of the evaluations to the students. Since the group members evaluate each other's performance throughout the exercise, we can identify those who take on leadership roles (and those who don't do their share of the work). Also, since students know that their group members evaluate them, they know they must be accountable to each other.

Results

Through the process described above, the instructor's grading load is diminished while the students' learning opportunities are enhanced. The students gain experience writing a scientific research paper and preparing a poster display, skills that will be required of them as professional scientists. This exemplifies the apprenticeship learning style, or learning by doing (Ritchie and Rigano 1996).

Students also gain experience working in collaborative groups and

> *We developed a writing exercise in which students replicate the work of professional scientists.*

assessing their peers' work. Recent publications have described the value of learning to work in groups and diminishing cut-throat competition among students (Bosworth 1994; Gokale 1995); this research paper and poster project does both.

In a traditional format, the primary authority rests with the instructor. Students work alone and seldom even see, and certainly never evaluate, the product of other students' work. Grades based solely on the instructor's evaluation of the work make the evaluation seem subjective. Since this writing project is group based and peer reviewed, it encourages students to respect their peers'

authority, the value of which is discussed by Barr and Tagg (1995). This exercise also gives students a perspective of their peer's work to compare to their own. It teaches them to read critically and to use constructive criticism as they rework drafts (Koprowski 1997).

Based on course evaluation comments, the students' major reservation concerns peer review. Nonetheless, they find the research paper and poster project one of the most rewarding experiences of the course. They like the opportunity to explore a topic in depth and to express their knowledge in a format different from exams and problem sets, adding to the diversity of skills they develop in the course.

References

Barr, R. B., and J. Tagg. 1995. From teaching to learning. *Change* (Nov-Dec): 13-25.

Bosworth, K. 1994. Developing collaborative skills in college students. *New Directions for Teaching and Learning* 59:25-30.

Gokale, A. A. 1995. Collaborative learning enhances critical thinking. *Journal of Technology Education* 7:22-27.

Holiday, W. 1994. The reading-science, learning-writing connection. *Journal of Research in Science Teaching* 31:877.

Jewett, Jr, J. W. 1991. Learning introductory physics through required writing. *Journal of College Science Teaching* 21:20.

Koprowski, J. L. 1997. Sharpening the craft of scientific writing. *Journal of College Science Teaching* 27:133.

Prain, V. 1996. Writing for learning in secondary science. *Teaching and Teacher Education* 12:609.

Ritchie, S. M., and D. L. Rigano. 1996. Laboratory apprenticeship through a student research project. *Journal of Research in Science Teaching* 33:799.

Trombulak, S. 1989. The real value of writing to learning in biology. *Journal of College Science Teaching* 18:384.

An Interactive Lecture Notebook—Twelve Ways to Improve Students' Grades

Drawing Students' Attention to What They Need to Know in Lecture

John E. Stencel

Much research supports the conclusion that most students do not take accurate and thorough notes. Hartley and Marshall (1974) reported that college freshman record as few as 11 percent of their instructor's critical lecture ideas. A study by Baker and Lombardi (1985) revealed that fewer than 25 percent of student note takers included propositions judged worthy of inclusion and only 50 percent listed main ideas.

The completeness of notes taken is also related to achievement. Students got higher grades if they took more thorough, complete notes, according to Locke (1977), and Collingwood and Hughes (1978) discovered better achievement if students were provided quality notes rather than personally recording them.

For several years students in general biology and anatomy and physiology courses at Olney Central College in Illinois have shown a preference for an

John E. Stencel is an instructor of life science, Olney Central College, 305 North West Street, Olney, IL 62450.

interactive lecture notebook. Some favorable student comments about the interactive lecture notebook include:

▲ "The interactive book was very good. It gave us time to learn and listen instead of trying to get all the notes down."

▲ "The notebook helped me get involved in the class."

▲ "When the notebooks came in late and we had to take notes in class I missed a lot. With the notebook I could concentrate better and got better grades on the lecture quizzes and pop quizzes."

▲ "I thought the notebooks were a big help. Sometimes it is so hard to take good notes and to know what the instructor thinks is important, with the notebooks it is all there."

The notebook is prepared on a computer so changes and corrections can be made easily. Students can purchase this booklet from the bookstore at cost ($7.25) at the beginning of the semester. The booklet is printed on a high-speed copier and contains a cover, table of contents, notes with illustrations, and sample quizzes compiled in a spiral binder. **Figure 1** shows the in-

teractive notebooks used in General Biology I and Human Anatomy and Physiology I and II (Stencel, 1995 a, b, c).

This interactive notebook has certain advantages over a didactic lecture approach where the teacher writes on a blackboard or overhead or does not write much at all. However, the blackboard and overhead are still available to add or illustrate information or make corrections. The twelve advantages of this interactive lecture notebook are:

(1) Notes are carefully organized in outline form, are easy to read, and are printed in various type sizes. Making notes available reduces student error in copying and spelling mistakes by the teacher. The sentences and phrases also track with the material presented. Many undergraduate students have poor note-taking skills, and this resource allows them to have good notes. Kiewra, Benton, and Lewis (1987) observed that students who took more thorough notes did better on tests although the class as a whole recorded only 37 percent of the total lecture

ideas presented. The authors of the study found that note taking was definitely related to achievement. Consequently, with low ability to encode and process information, students took less elaborate or accurate notes and got poorer grades. In addition, research supports that students who listen to a lecture and review the instructor's notes are generally more successful academically than are students who take and review their own notes (Kiewra, 1987). The interactive notebook should help students improve their test scores and final grades.

(2) Time and effort is saved in lecture presentations since teachers and students spend less of both on writing. Also, students can concentrate on what is being presented instead of worrying about keeping up on note taking (Wilson, 1994; Collison, 1992). This extra time (some 15-20 minutes per 50-minute lecture period) can be used for recitations, problem solving, critical thinking, student questions, and the presentation of new, current material.

(3) The notes are interactive and thus involve student participation. In some places there are blank spaces so students can fill in answers in class or label drawings. Students are required to bring four colored pencils (red, green, black, and blue) so they can color their predrawn diagrams, illustrations, and drawings. For emphasis they might underline certain words, color a cell, or color code the body cavities of a human. For example, with an illustration of major body cavities and subcavities, the teacher shows an enlarged overhead drawing and color codes it with the students. Using the color markers, Devine (1987) recommends underlining main ideas, circling new terms or key words, drawing arrows to connect ideas, and using stars to indicate important ideas. These marks are incorporated into the interactive notebook by the students.

The teacher can ask students questions about the material presented. If students are paying attention, they should be able to give an answer based on the notes. The instructor can also ask other questions pertaining to the material not included in the notebook and these answers must be incorporated in the notes. In a class of fewer than 25 students, interaction can take place with every student in the class. In biology, a discussion might center on the adaptation of certain organisms that aid in fitting into a particular environmental niche. The teacher might list some adaptations of a cactus to its desert environment and ask students to add to the list. For homework, the teacher could ask for adaptations of a flea, a white tail deer, or humans. Students would write these in their notebooks and discuss them during the next lecture period.

(4) The interactive lecture notebook includes quick study and review preparation from the last lecture period. At the end of the lecture, students are asked to answer questions distributed throughout the notes and report their responses at the next class session. The questions may involve summarizing or integrating the lecture material or may require that students search their textbook or reference material in the library. Occasionally, a short pop quiz is given in the next class session on the material previously covered. This quiz promotes better attendance since quizzes cannot be made up and causes most students to study every day instead of cramming the for hour-length exams. Hartley (1983) and Kiewra (1985a) reviewed 24 studies that showed if students continually review their notes, they succeed better on tests.

(5) The interactive notebook allows space to add updated material. Each page of the interactive notebook has a two-inch outer margin for extra notes, illustrations, or cross references to the

lab or textbook. In science, new developments occur daily, so this room gives the instructor a place to add current material. Students can use the space to summarize points, add related text, reference material, and so on. Wilson (1994) also uses space margins to include "reminders of points of clarification and additional examples that you wish to include at the last minute."

(6) The notebook also includes handouts and study sheets that complement the lecture material so that students can participate in the learning process. For example, the teacher presents the major stages and events of cellular respiration; then students fill in the blanks, matching which event occurs at which stage, such as listing the stages that make ATP, stating which stage is aerobic or anaerobic, and so on.

(7) One of the purposes of science is to think quantitatively. Thus, simple mathematics is used to solve problems related to the concepts taught. Problem strategies are listed in the interactive notebook and simple problems already included are worked out during the lecture. Also, the teacher can give new problems that students can work out during the lecture with the help of the instructor. Knowledgeable students can act as tutors to those around them who are having difficulty working out the problems. This way, students receive instant feedback to see if they really understand the problems. More sets of problems are given for homework to be covered the next class session.

(8) The notebook is a great aid for students who are absent or late for class. The notes are legible, cohesive, inclusive, and follow a logical sequence of events. This is much better than getting illegible, incorrect, or incomplete notes from a fellow student. Collison (1992) observed that some students

who missed class were reluctant to borrow notes or did not know anyone from whom they could borrow them. In a Kiewra (1985b) study, some absentee students who obtained their instructor's notes did better on exams than students who were in class taking their own notes.

(9) Since the material is already printed and accessible to students before the lecture, a student could read the notes, relate them to the textbook material, and be better prepared in class (Wilson, 1994).

(10) The interactive notebook can save money for a school. Instead of passing out handouts, articles, and practice quizzes at school expense, the students can buy the material at the bookstore at cost.

(11) At the end of each unit is a multiple-choice practice quiz. Students review these questions and the teacher gives the answers in a later class.

(12) The interactive notebook is a creative personal accumulation of biological facts and concepts from books, journals, workshops, meetings, and experiences. Each teacher should have his or her unique approach to biology within the framework of recent textbooks or current, widely accepted syllabi. Some students believe that printed notes improve their grades because their own notes are incomplete; better notes should produce better grades (Collison, 1992). According to Kiewra (1996) the interactive notebook could be analogous to an information-processing model. This model involves the processes of selective attention, encoding (coding information into usable form), placement of information into short-term memory, storage in long-term memory, and retrieval from memory. A breakdown in any of these processes usually leads to a loss of memory or no memory at all. The

Figure 1. Interactive notebooks used in Olney Central College's biology, anatomy, and physiology courses. The notebooks provide students with complete and accurate lecture material, allowing information to be incorporated into their long-term memory.

notebook helps students to listen better rather than putting much of their attention to reading the board and writing down information; it prevents an overload of short-term memory by avoiding confusion in trying to write and comprehend information simultaneously.

This notebook increases selective attention to what is important and of consequence. The notes themselves, of course, are a form of external storage that unlike memory is resistant to losing (forgetting) information. Answering questions and organizing notes reinforces meaningful information, allowing material to be incorporated into long-term memory. ❏

Acknowledgments

The author would like to thank Dr. Kenneth Kiewra of Nebraska State University and Professor David Cunningham of Olney Central College (OCC) for reviewing and improving this manuscript, Fran Stencel, director of the Learning Resources Center, and business professor Ken Allen, both of OCC, for their proofreading, and Jane Marriott, public information specialist at OCC, for her photograph.

References

Baker, L., and B.R. Lombardi. 1985. Students' lecture notes and their relation to test performance. *Teaching of Psychology* 12(1): 28-32.

Collingwood, V., and D.C. Hughes. 1978. Effects of three types of university lecture notes on student achievement. *Journal of Educational Psychology* 70:175-179.

Collison, M. 1992. Sale of class notes: A new skirmish over an old idea. *The Chronicle of Higher Education* 38(April 8): 35-6.

Devine, T.G. 1987. *Teaching Studying Skills: A Guide for Teachers*. 2nd ed. Boston: Allyn and Bacon.

Hartley, J., and S. Marshall. 1974. On notes and note taking. *University Quarterly* 28:225-235.

Hartley, J. 1983. Note taking research: Resetting the scoreboard. *Bulletin of the British Psychological Society* 36:13-14.

Kiewra, K.A. 1985a. Investigating note taking and review: A depth of processing alternative. *Educational Psychologist* 20:20-23.

Kiewra, K.A. 1985b. Learning from a lecture: An investigation of note taking, review, and attendance at a lecture. *Human Learning* 4: 73-77.

Kiewra, K.A. 1987. Note taking and review: The research and its implications. *Instructional Science* 16:233-249.

Kiewra, K.A., S.L. Benton, and L.B. Lewis. 1987. Qualitative aspects of note taking and their relationship with information-processing ability and academic achievement. *Journal of Instructional Psychology* 14(Sept.): 110-117.

Kiewra, K.A. 1996. Personal Communication. University of Nebraska, Teachers College, Lincoln, Nebraska.

Locke, E.A. 1977. An empirical study of lecture note taking among college students. *Journal of Education Research* 71:93-99.

Stencel, J.E. 1995a. *An Interactive Lecture Notebook-Notes From LSC 1101 General Biology I.* Olney, Illinois: Illinois Eastern Community Colleges Press.

Stencel, J.E. 1995b. *An Interactive Lecture Notebook-Notes from LSC 2111 Human Anatomy and Physiology I.* Olney, Illinois: Illinois Eastern Community Colleges Press.

Stencel, J.E. 1995c. *An Interactive Lecture Notebook-Notes from LSC 2112 Human Anatomy and Physiology II.* Olney, Illinois: Illinois Eastern Community Colleges Press.

Wilson, R.W. 1994. A method to facilitate note taking by students. *Journal of College Science Teaching* 23(4): 233-234.

Using E-mail to Improve Communication in the Introductory Science Classroom

An Excellent Tool for Encouraging Students to Enter Into Conversation with the Instructor and Each Other

Kathryn Hedges and Barbara Mania-Farnell

Large lecture classes tend to produce an atmosphere of competition and seldom encourage cooperation among students. Additionally, it is difficult to establish student-instructor interaction in these types of courses. A few students will interact with the instructor during or after class; however, the majority of students sit silently through lectures and quickly depart afterwards.

Strauss and Fulwiler (1987, 1989-1990) promote writing as a means of communication between students and faculty. They suggest that students should write notes to the instructor about problems encountered in interpretation of material in the text and in lectures. The notes can be used in class as a framework for discussion.

E-mail can be used to extend this concept by providing a tool that can improve student-instructor interaction and create an atmosphere of instructor support. Electronic communication also provides an opportunity to address a student's individual problems. The use of e-mail has been tried in the human biology course at Indiana University Northwest, a commuter campus.

The human biology course attracts a wide range of students. Some have little or no science background and are taking this course to fulfill a general requirement. Other students have strong science backgrounds and are taking the course as a review or to fulfill requirements for programs that will lead to careers in the allied health fields.

A portion of the students, particularly in the former group, are affected by the issue of science phobia, and a number of them have not learned the study skills necessary for success in the sciences. Many of the students work 20 to 40 hours per week, and some have families. With this great diversity in backgrounds and experience it is important to find a method that involves all students in discussion of the course material. It is also important to provide students with a supportive atmosphere, one which minimizes competition and maximizes the use of cooperative and interactive methods (Seymour 1992; Hoots 1992).

THE ASSIGNMENTS

Sixty-two students who were initially enrolled in the human biology course were asked to apply for e-mail accounts on the first day of class. At this time, and again at the end of the semester, they were surveyed to determine their experience with computers and attitudes toward employing e-mail in the class. Their first assignment, designed to introduce the use of e-mail, was to send an e-mail message about their background to the instructor. All the students, in turn,

Kathryn Hedges is a science educator at Ensweiler Academy, 6111 W. Ridge Road, Gary, IN 46408; e-mail: khedges@lakeridge.K12.in.us; and Barbara Mania-Farnell is an assistant professor in the department of biological sciences, Purdue University Calumet, Hammond, IN 46323; e-mail: bmania@calumet.purdue.edu.

received an e-mail response from the instructor.

After being introduced to e-mail operations, students were given several different assignments throughout the semester. Responses to the assignments were sent to the instructor via e-mail. Students earned points toward the fi-

---

Redirecting students' work through e-mail helped the students work out misconceptions at their own pace, and also helped the instructor identify areas that needed to be covered further in class.

---

nal grade for each completed assignment. The assignment sets were as follows:

Students were given packets containing current articles and news briefs from journals and science magazines. The articles dealt with topics that were related to course material. The students were asked to read and then discuss the articles by e-mail. Communicating by e-mail provided a means of extending the curriculum to include current events and applications without taking time from the classroom. Students did not have to read all the articles in the packet.
▲ News briefs from Science News included: 1.) "Cow's Milk: New Link to Diabetes?" (1996) 2.) "Contraceptive Concerns About HIV" (1996) 3.) "Drug Wards Off Sickle-Cell Attacks" (1995) 4.) "Memorable Debate: Do Old Brain Cells Die?" (1996) 5.) "Cow's Milk Not Linked to Early Diabetes" (1996).
▲ Articles included: 1.) "Experts Wary of Ever-Changing Influenza A Virus" (Pennisi 1996) 2.) "Forever Smart: Does Estrogen Enhance Memory?" (Fackelmann 1995) 3.) "A Conversa-

tion with David Satcher" (Campbell 1996) 4.) "Dyslexia" (Shaywitz 1996) 5.) "Neural Code Breakers: What Language Do Neurons Use to Communicate?" (Lipkin 1996).

Students were assigned critical thinking questions that related to classroom topics. They were to answer these via e-mail. Eight problems were assigned during the semester. Some of these included:
▲ Astronaut Mark Vallor was a little nervous as he awaited his orders to board the spacecraft. As part of his final physical before liftoff his blood pressure was taken. Mark was lying down. Once in space the measurement was repeated. Remember there is no gravity in space. Would you expect his blood pressure to be higher, lower, or the same with respect to the first measurement. Explain.
▲ Flirtatious Fay was an avid jogger. During one of her morning runs on the beach she met Maximus, a muscular weight lifter. Maximus flirted with Fay who was not impressed by his brawn. She continued to jog down the beach, with Maximus jogging along for about a half mile at which time he was forced to quit due to fatigue. How is it that Fay could outrun Maximus despite the fact that she is less muscular?
▲ Grandma Jackson has been going to the same dressmaker for thirty years. She always has her skirt length adjusted to twenty inches. Lately however, the skirts seem to be much longer. Grandma complains that the

dressmaker's new assistant does not know how to use a ruler correctly. When the dressmaker rechecked the measurement it was exactly 20 inches. Explain what has happened.

Students were also assigned group activities. In this situation they were given a simple experiment that could be done at home. They were then to discuss and evaluate their results with group members via e-mail and send an overall report to the instructor. Background information for the experiment was discussed in class. Two of the group activities included:
▲ Students were given three tubes of 3% agarose. Two tubes contained one ml of crystal violet at the top and one tube contained one ml of methyl green at the top. The students were to take the tubes home. One of the tubes containing crystal violet was to be placed in the refrigerator and the other tubes were to be left at room temperature. The students were to observe the tubes and write a discussion on diffusion and how it is affected by time and temperature based on the results obtained by group members.
▲ Students were told to take uncooked chicken bones and either bake them or soak them in vinegar. They were then to observe what happened to the bones and write a group report on bone composition.

RESULTS

The use of e-mail in the human biology classroom was originally proposed to increase student-instructor interaction. This happened. However, several other beneficial outcomes also resulted. These included:

Increased student-instructor interaction built student confidence.

Among the assignments students were to undertake were reading and discussing via e-mail the current articles and news briefs. Two benefits emerged from this assignment. First, the packet material reinforced classroom lectures and allowed the students to see the relevance of classroom information in relation to "the real world."

For instance, one student observed that she never realized how much processing takes place in the brain until she read "Neural Code Breakers." In particular she linked this to driving: "I never thought of there being a lot of information for my brain to sort out. I just drive and it's such an automatic thing. Most of these articles raise thoughts that wouldn't have occurred to me. It feels good to be using my brain."

Second, a number of students related the material to personal experiences and initiated a discussion with the instructor to obtain answers to questions of importance to them. For example, one student asked and then examined the question of why we recover from measles, mumps, and the flu but not from HIV. Another student asked if there was a correlation between HIV and sickle cell disease, since two of the articles she read indicated a higher rate of these diseases in the African population than other groups.

Although students probably make connections between class material and the real world/personal experiences in the classroom, these supplemental e-mail assignments appeared to help students make these connections. In turn, this resulted in increased understanding and retention of classroom material.

Critical thinking questions encourage students to consider information that they have learned in class and to apply the information to different situations to solve problems. E-mail proved to be a practical way for students to respond to the critical thinking questions.

In past semesters these types of questions have been assigned in the human biology course, although students answered them on paper. In comparison to paper answers, we found that e-mail responses were much shorter and to the point. This is an important aspect when instructors need to grade large numbers of student assignments. This may be partly because students were able to get further clarification if they were not sure what the question was asking.

The main benefit for the students was that they were allowed time and given direction to develop their answers. In the past, primarily due to grading volume, if students answered incorrectly their papers were returned with a low score. With e-mail it is much easier to engage students, prompting them if necessary, in a discussion until they work their way to the correct answer. This is more beneficial then giving the students a low score and then the answer.

A few initial answers for the question on Fay and Maximus are given below.

> The reason Fay is able to outrun Maximus, even though Fay is less muscular, is that it takes a lot of gas to run a bigger engine. With Maximus' muscles and mass he became fatigued a lot quicker because his body demands more energy to operate then does Fays'.
>
> It doesn't matter how muscular you are when running. You can be muscular and lift weights everyday but not work on your cardiovascular system, which helps you to run farther. Since Fay is an avid jogger, her cardiovascular system is conditioned for jogging and Max's is not.
>
> One of the body's most distinguishing characteristics is the muscles' ability to transform energy into directed mechanical energy. In so doing muscle becomes capable of exerting force, allowing Fay to outrun Max.

In our case, the appropriate answer, combined with material that was covered in class, needed to include a discussion of muscle structure and in particular muscle fiber type. Students were reminded, via e-mail, to rethink their answers keeping this in mind.

Finally, group projects were assigned early in the semester. These projects required that students work together and share information outside of class. Students could meet in person or via e-mail. In this course the majority of groups met in person, primarily because most did not have access to computers at home. However, students with tight schedules did find communication through e-mail advantageous.

After group assignments were completed, each student was required to respond individually to the instructor with the results of the experiments conducted by that group and an interpretation of those results. As in the previous section, when problems arose students were redirected through e-mail responses and, when necessary, further discussion was pursued in class.

Although most students did not have difficulty with their discussion on diffusion, as this topic was well covered in class, the few that did received additional instructions via e-mail. For example, one group e-mailed the following message: "We have come to the conclusion that the process used is active. We feel this way because the solute is using energy to move through the jelly-like substance. We also feel that the green molecule is bigger because it moved further then the purple."

Surprisingly, many students had misconceptions as to why baked chicken bones break whereas those soaked in vinegar bend, e.g. "...Our group found that when liquid was added to the bone it served as a lubricant and kept the bone easy to move so that it would not break. When liquid was removed the bones were brittle and easy to break." Little time was spent on the chemical properties of bone in class, but as a result of students' answers this topic was revisited, using chalk and beef jerky to illustrate properties of substances with different chemical compositions.

In these assignments, as with those discussed in the preceding paragraphs, e-mail redirection helped the students work out misconceptions at their own pace, and also helped the instructor

Providing a supportive atmosphere that minimizes competition and maximizes the use of cooperative and interactive methods eases students' fear of using computers.

identify areas that needed to be covered further in class.

Overall, working with students via e-mail increased student-instructor interaction; a similar phenomenon has been noted by Collins (1997) who used an electronic bulletin board. E-mail also helped the students feel more comfortable about asking questions. Some student comments include:

"Computer communication brought me into technology (I was sheltered). I think using e-mail is the best way to communicate with professors. You have an opportunity to share how you feel about something without seeing the reaction on the face of the professor. E-mail bridged the gap between the professor and the students. I thought that it made the professor more approachable and more down to earth."

"I really enjoyed the e-mailing in this class....I really think it was a way to constantly keep me thinking of the class and the material. The articles were great."

"I initially hated the whole idea. Now I think it is a good idea. It helped me to become more computer literate. I felt more comfortable at first talking to you via computer than face to face; now that we have talked by way of e-mail several times I am a lot more comfortable with you in person."

E-mail communication enhanced student writing.

Studies on curriculum support the idea that writing improves retention time of learned material (Piak and Norris 1983), and that structured writing helps students organize their thought processes (Kirkpatrick and Pittendrigh 1984).

The postulates set forth for writing include: 1.) writing yields a permanent record of thoughts that allows the author to rethink and revise the material; 2.) writing requires greater organization than speech and must be more explicit to retain the meaning beyond the initial context; 3.) writing encourages the incorporation of new ideas into existing knowledge; and 4.) writing is an active process integrating several modalities: the hand, the eye, and the brain (Emig 1977; Griffin 1983; Applebee 1984).

In conjunction with the above, Randy Moore (1994) has found that when students use writing as a tool to learn biology, their involvement and mastery of the subject increases. The

use of writing also encourages student creativity and in-depth analysis of problems.

An additional benefit of using e-mail in the human biology classroom was that the amount of writing students did increased considerably. The average number of words written per student was 2,259 (although the amount did vary between students), equivalent to a short term paper. While the writing style tended to be informal, it did lend itself to expression of thought, generation of ideas, and exchange of views. Increased writing should help students develop their writing skills and improve their retention of material.

Increased student confidence in computer technology.

Students were surveyed about their attitudes toward using e-mail in the classroom and about computer usage in general. At the beginning of the course 16 percent of the students reported that they used a computer often, 44 percent reported that they used a computer occasionally, and 40 percent stated that they used a computer seldom or never. Only 14 percent of the students had used e-mail prior to taking the course.

Despite their lack of experience, many students had positive attitudes about using e-mail as part of the course. Sixty percent were positive at the beginning of the semester and 86 percent felt positive about the idea by the end of the semester. The majority of students, 80 percent, reported that they planned to continue using e-mail, 12 percent were not sure, and eight percent said that they would not use e-mail except as a future course requirement.

The majority of the students who described having a negative attitude at first about using e-mail were concerned with the amount of work involved in learning how to use e-mail. One student wrote, "I was initially against the idea because I thought that it would be a big hassle. After I learned how easy e-mail was to use, I think it is a great way to communicate with others, especially hard-to-contact professors...."

Another wrote that "at first I wasn't thrilled about the e-mail. I had never used it. I didn't like the idea of trying to figure it out and looking like a dummy. Once I learned how to use it, I really enjoyed it. I think it was a great idea that it was required because I never would have done it otherwise." Students who reported negative attitudes at the end of the course generally had difficulty using computers at the university. They primarily reported time constraints.

Students can learn to use e-mail with no formal instruction. Some students may feel initial resistance to the idea, but, in most cases, they enjoy the use of e-mail and computers once they learn how to use them. Providing a reason to learn how to use e-mail in an entry level course should benefit the students, as e-mail is widely used as a form of communication in our society.

In addition, it seems likely that those students who are less familiar with computers will benefit by increased computer usage. As one student wrote: "I've never used a computer in class before in my life and I have concluded that I should become more familiar with computers because of the things I now know." Another student even decided "I think I want to learn to use the Internet also."

CONCLUSION

Many students liked to communicate frequently with the instructor via e-mail. As one wrote, "I really enjoyed e-mail because it was a great way to communicate with you and it was more personal. If a person was too embarrassed to ask a question in class, they had the option to be discreet and

e-mail you with the question or comment." Others commented that by using e-mail they "didn't need to compete with everyone else to get a question answered," and that e-mail "made the professor more approachable and more down to earth."

The comments of students on their surveys indicated that students who are shy or unable to pose a question during class time find e-mail a valuable means of communication. "...It is sometimes easier to find time outside of class to ask lengthy questions or discuss subjects outside the realm of the class." The speed with which responses are possible truly makes e-mail a practical instrument for discussion.

In terms of grading, the use of e-mail also proved to be efficient, particularly when compared to grading written assignments. With e-mail, assignments did not have to be collected and it was possible to respond to students as they turned in their answers, rather than having them wait until an entire set was graded. In general, since not all students answered on the same day, at most one to two hours per day of instructor time, either at the office or at home, was sufficient to respond to all student comments.

An additional benefit of e-mail was that if students had questions they either e-mailed them to the instructor or, if they needed to discuss the questions in person, they usually e-mailed to set up an interview time, as opposed to just dropping in. This actually turned out to be more efficient for the instructor since students were less likely to stop by during research hours or lecture preparation time.

Overall, e-mail promotes the use of computer technology. E-mail also provides a way to encourage students to write about topics discussed in class. This, in turn, helps students think more formally about these topics and

gives them a greater opportunity to relate them to their own experiences. Finally, e-mail is an excellent tool for individualizing instruction and encouraging students to enter into conversation with the instructor. This is especially useful in classes with a diverse student population.

Acknowledgments
This work was supported in part by an Indiana University Northwest Writing Across the Curriculum Mini Grant to K. Hedges.

References
Applebee, A. N. 1984. Writing and reasoning. *Review of Educational Research* 54:577-596.

Campbell, N. A. 1996. A conversation with David Satcher. *The American Biology Teacher* 58:353-358.

Collins, M. A. J. 1997. A successful experiment with an electronic bulletin board in a large class. *Journal of College Science Teaching* 26:189-191.

Emig, J. 1997. Writing as a mode of learning. *College Composition and Communications* 28:122-128.

Fackelmann, K. 1995. Forever smart: Does estrogen enhance memory? *Science News* 147:74-75.

Griffin, C. W. 1983. A process to critical thinking using writing to teach many disciplines. *Improving College and University Teaching* 31:121-128.

Hoots, R. 1992. An outsider's insights on neglected issues in science education. *Journal of College Science Teaching* 21:300-304.

Kirkpatrick, L., and A. Pittendrigh. 1984. A writing teacher in the physics classroom. *The Physics Teacher* 22:159-164.

Lipkin, R. 1996. Neural code breakers: What language do neurons use to communicate? *Science News* 149:392-393.

Moore, R. 1994. Writing to learn biology. *Journal of College Science Teaching* 23:289-295.

Pennisi, E. 1996. Experts wary of ever-changing Influenza A virus. *ASM News* 262:356-360.

Piak, M. K., and E. M. Norris. 1983. Writing to learn in statistics, mathematics, and computer science. In *Writing to Learn: Essays and Reflections on Writing Across the Curriculum*, ed. C. Thaiss. Dubuque, IA: Kendall/Hunt.

Seymour, E. 1992. Undergraduate problems with teaching and advising in SME majors—Explaining gender differences in attrition rates. *Journal of College Science Teaching* 21:284-292.

Shaywitz, S. E. 1996. Dyslexia. *Scientific American* 275:98-104.

Strauss, M., and T. Fulwiler. 1987. Interactive writing and learning chemistry. *Journal of College Science Teaching* 16:256-262.

Strauss, M., and T. Fulwiler. 1989-90. Writing to learn in large lecture classes. *Journal of College Science Teaching* 19:158-163.

Using Internet Class Notes and PowerPoint in the Physical Geology Lecture

Comparing the Success of Computer Technology With Traditional Teaching Techniques

Erwin J. Mantei

In recent years, a number of studies have been conducted to compare the effectiveness of computer technology in teaching with that of traditional educational techniques. As most readers would undoubtedly conclude, the results of these studies strongly favored computer technology.

In 1994, Fifield and Peifer found that the use of computer-based images in two introductory college biology courses helped students to better understand the material presented to them. Also in 1994, a study by Pearson et al. indicated that knowledge retention of materials by students was greater with the use of multimedia presentations than with traditional ones.

Erwin J. Mantei is a professor of geology and geochemistry in the geography, geology and planning department, Southwest Missouri State University, Springfield, MO 65804; e-mail: ejm893f@mail.smsu.edu.

This finding was followed in 1995 by an analysis by Jensen et al. in which the researchers discovered that students exposed to computer presentations in lecture sections on diffusion and osmosis scored higher on posttests than those in control sections. Most recently, in 1999, Privateer, in summarizing the use of computer technology in the classroom, came to essentially the same conclusions. All of these findings are compatible with detailed research done at Southwest Missouri Sate University (SMSU) using data from the period 1992 to 1998.

PARAMETERS OF THE SMSU STUDY

The context of the SMSU study was a physical geology course, a general education requirement. The majority of the students enrolled in the course were not majoring in a science discipline, but they constituted a representative cross section of the various academic programs offered at SMSU. A laboratory component of this course was not included in the study.

The SMSU study compared student performance in physical geology lecture classes using a traditional method of presentation with that using Internet notes and PowerPoint lecture slides. In the traditional method, topic notes were presented in an outlined form on the board. Overhead transparencies were used to supplement topic material. No other visual technology was used. Student exam scores obtained from the traditional method represent the control for this study and include data from 10 semester classes between 1992 and 1996. Scores from four semester classes from 1997 to 1998 represent the test group. The average number of students per class for the control semesters was 74.3 and 67.0 for the test semesters.

METHODOLOGY

▲ *Similar Class Activities for the Research Groups*

The number of variables in the control and test groups were held to a minimum. For all semester classes, both groups featured:

Table 1. Physical geology lecture exam. A comparison of physical geology lecture exam scores of the control group (1992-1996) with that of the test group (1997 to 1998).

Spring Semester				Fall Semester			
Year	Exam	Median Exam Score	Number of Students	Year	Exam	Median Exam Score	Number of Students
1992	1	66	87	1992	1	70	86
	2	73			2	69	
	3	70			3	71	
	4	70			4	73	
Mean		69.8		Mean		70.8	
1993	1	69	91	1993	1	73	74
	2	73			2	69	
	3	76			3	70	
	4	71			4	73	
Mean		72.3		Mean		71.3	
1994	1	71	81	1994	1	73	71
	2	69			2	73	
	3	68			3	70	
	4	73			4	69	
Mean		70.3		Mean		71.3	
1995	1	70	64	1995	1	66	68
	2	71			2	74	
	3	68			3	76	
	4	71			4	70	
Mean		70		Mean		71.5	
1996	1	69	60	1996	1	72	61
	2	71			2	76	
	3	70			3	70	
	4	72			4	71	
Mean		70.5		Mean		72.3	
1997	1	76	53	1997	1	75	70
	2	76			2	80	
	3	77			3	72	
	4	75			4	80	
Mean		76.3		Mean		76.8	
1998	1	76	75	1998	1	74	70
	2	76			2	78	
	3	77			3	76	
	4	75			4	76	
Mean		75		Mean		76	

1. The same class policy statement and calendar of class activities. (Using the same calendar assured equal presentation length for each topic.)

2. Identical lecture topics, sequence taught by the same instructor, and class topics presented in the same outline form with the same supplementary materials.

3. Identical exam questions.

4. Identical practice exams. (These exams allowed students to evaluate their knowledge of the material prior to each major exam.)

5. The same textbook.

An interactive CD-ROM was available to some students in the test group but none in the control group.

This variable is addressed later in this study.

▲ *Conversion of Class Materials into Internet Notes and PowerPoint Slides*

The research that shows the benefits of computers and multimedia in the classroom has been followed by studies that have determined that animated software programs can also strengthen student learning (Williamson and Abraham 1995; Palmiter 1991). In particular, studies indicate that animated software helps students to experience text, images, motion, and sound (Janda 1992), a necessary advantage in the field of physical geology. Like Nantz and

Lundgren (1998), who found PowerPoint to be an excellent software package for presenting material in the classroom, we, too, relied on PowerPoint lecture slides for our course.

All lecture notes and practice exams used in the classes representing the control group were converted to HTML and placed on the Internet. Internet notes included detailed material in outline form with supplements such as figures, tables, and illustrations from the textbook and links to other web sites. The textbook publisher granted permission to use the supplements.

Access to other web sites allowed the student to obtain more information about a concept or to view the concept from a different perspective. Many of these web sites included physical geology courses offered at other universities. Lecture class presentations in animated PowerPoint format with sound effects were prepared using the Internet notes as a guide. Information on the PowerPoint slides was a condensed version of the text portion of the Internet notes and included all of the same textbook supplements.

All PowerPoint lecture slides prepared for the classroom were also added to the same web site as the Internet notes. The URL for the web site is: http://courses.smsu.edu/ejm893f/creative/index.html.

All material at the above web site location was first made available to the students enrolled in the physical geology lecture class in the spring semester of 1997. Students were encouraged to obtain a hard copy from the computer, read the appropriate material before class, and bring the copy to class. They could supplement this material with their own notes taken in class. These preliminary steps allowed the students to actively participate in the class. Emerson and Mosteller (1998) state that students need to be active participants in the education process to benefit from it.

Near the end of each semester, the students in each test group completed an identical questionnaire (see Appendix). They were asked to compare the use of Internet notes and class presentation in PowerPoint format with that of various traditional forms of presentations used in their other classes. The questionnaire was designed to rate the desirability of Internet notes and lecture presentations in PowerPoint format. The total number of student responses on each question from the four test groups ranged from 242 to 248. Students were asked to rate each question between 1 and 10.

RESULTS AND DISCUSSION

▲ Class Survey

Students rated questions 1 and 2, 9.3 and 8.3, respectively, indicating that they find class material presented in animated PowerPoint format more interesting than traditional lecture formats. It also appears that students believed they could learn material better if it was presented in a PowerPoint format.

Students rated questions 3 and 4, 9.4 and 9.5, respectively. They felt it was easier to learn presented materials if classnotes were available to them, and accessing notes on the Internet was more desirable than obtaining them from the library or other sources. When students were asked why Internet notes were more desirable, the most common answer was that they were more accessible. Another answer to this question was that the topic supplements to other web sites were available with Internet notes and, after viewing the notes on the computer, students could obtain copies of the supplementary material.

Students in the test group classes would bring Internet notes to class and supplement them with notes taken during the lecture. With minimum note taking, they felt they could listen to the instructor more intently. A total of 226 responses from the test group indicated that 87 percent of the responding students brought Internet notes to class for use there and 10 percent used them outside of class. Of these two groups, 95 percent accessed the notes from the computer and printed a copy while five percent made copies from another student's notes.

Questions 5 and 6 were rated 9.2 and 8.4, respectively. Students believed that the use of Internet notes combined with the presentation of lecture material in the PowerPoint format improved the overall learning environment. Furthermore, they felt that

Table 2. The percent letter grade for spring (S) and fall (F) semesters for the control group (1992-1996) and test group (1997-1998).

		Percent Letter Grade					
Year	Semester	A	B	C	D	F	N*
1992	S	18	26	26	20	7	3
	F	16	28	25	14	8	9
1993	S	14	31	31	9	5	10
	F	18	18	30	13	17	4
1994	S	13	25	34	14	5	9
	F	11	20	37	11	17	4
1995	S	9	18	28	19	8	18
	F	21	24	15	12	18	10
1996	S	22	26	17	14	14	7
	F	8	30	24	17	13	8
1997	S	19	38	20	6	11	6
	F	20	34	27	9	6	4
1998	S	15	37	21	13	9	5
	F	13	37	28	8	10	4

*dropped class prior to assigned grade.

Table 3. The percent letter grade distribution in the control and test groups.

Letter Grade	Mean (%) of Control Group	Mean(%) of Test Group
A	15	16.8
B	24.6	36.5*
C	26.7	24.0
D	14.3	9.0
F	11.2	9.0
N**	8.1	4.8

* t test indicates significant difference at the 0.01% alpha level
** dropped class prior to assigned grade

Internet notes were more useful than PowerPoint slides for learning material.

▲ *Student Performance*

As mentioned above, identical exam questions were used in each class representing the control and test groups. **Table 1** shows exam scores for the semesters representing the control and test groups. There is a significant increase in the exam scores starting in the spring semester of 1997 with the first test group. Higher exam scores continued in the remaining classes representing the test group. The mean scores for all exams in the control and test groups were 71.0 and 76.2, respectively.

A "t" test comparing scores of both groups indicates a significant difference in the exam scores on the 0.001% alpha level. The change in letter grade associated with the increase in number grade was determined. Exam scores for each student in each semester for each of the four exams in the control and test groups were assigned a letter grade based on a common grading scale: 90% or > = A; 80%-89.99% = B; 70%-79% = C; 60%-69.99% = D; 60% or < = F. **Table 2** shows the percent letter grade distribution for each semester class for the control and test groups. An N grade represents withdrawal from the class in an appropriate time frame prior to grade assignments for the course.

From the data in Table 2, the mean percent letter grade for each class in the control and test groups was determined. **Table 3** shows an increase percent in A and B grades in the test group and a decrease in C, D, F, and N grades. A "t" test indicates the percent B grade in the test group compared to the control group is significantly different at the 0.02% alpha level.

From the data in Table 2 and use of a "t" test, the sum of the percent A and B grades in the test group is higher and significantly different than the

Table 4. Comparison of student ACT scores and mean exam scores for the control (1994-1996) and test groups (1997 to 1998).

Year/Semester		Mean ACT Scores		Mean Exam Scores
		Composite	Science	
1994	S*	21.5	22.1	70.3
	F**	21.7	22.1	71.3
1995	S	22.4	22.4	70.0
1996	S	22.1	22.0	70.5
	F	21.3	21.2	72.3
1997	S	22.5	22.1	76.3
	F	21.9	22.2	76.8
1998	S	22.3	22.4	75.0
	F	22.5	22.4	76.0

* Spring Semester
** Fall Semester

same for the control at the 0.02% alpha level. In a similar comparison, the sum of the percent of D and F grades are lower and significantly different at the 5% alpha level.

Higher student ACT scores in a class may result in higher exam scores. **Table 4** shows a comparison of student ACT scores and associated mean exam scores for students in the control and test groups. The ACT scores are not available for 1992-1993 inclusive and the fall semester of 1995. Composite and science ACT scores are both reported. The mean composite and science scores for the control group are 21.8 and 22, respectively. The associated mean exam score is 71.0. The mean composite and science scores for the test group are each 22.3 with an associated mean exam score of 76.2. The ACT scores appear to be quite similar for the control and test groups. Thus, this similarity would not appear to account for a higher mean exam score in the test group.

The increase in exam scores associated with the test group could be attributed to an improved teaching performance by the instructor, but this is not the case here. Students evaluated their instructor at the end of each se-

mester using the same evaluation form in the control and test groups. Results from the evaluation indicated there was no difference in the quality of teaching performance by the same instructor during the semesters for the test group compared to the same for the control.

A CD-ROM associated with the textbook was available to the students in all but the first semester class of the test group but not for the control group. Students were encouraged to use the interactive CD-ROM. The substantial increase in exam scores in the test group appeared one semester prior to the introduction of the CD-ROM. Also, the exam scores did not increase with the use of the CD-Rom. Thus, it seems clear that the introduction of the CD-ROM did not affect the substantial increase in exam scores representing the test group.

CONCLUSION

The higher exam scores associated with the test group appear to result from the introduction of Internet notes and PowerPoint lecture presentations in the classroom. Students in the test group enjoyed the PowerPoint lecture presentations and felt the

Internet notes helped them to learn the material better than the traditional presentations used in other classes. These students performed better on exams than those in the control group, reinforcing Pearson et al.'s (1994) results that show students learn more when they enjoy the method of presentation.

Our study, which indicates that Internet notes available to students and the use of PowerPoint slides for lectures are a more efficient way of presenting class materials that take 20 percent less time than traditional techniques, supports the research by Campbell et al. (1995) and Leonard (1992) that found computer-supported methods used in the classroom have the potential to increase learner performance and decrease instructor time. ∎

References

Campbell, J. O., C. A. Lison, T. K. Borsook, J. A. Hoover, and P. H. Arnold. 1995. Using computer and video technologies to develop interpersonal skills. *Computer in Human Behavior* 11:223-239.

Emerson, J. D., and F. Mosteller. 1998. Interactive multimedia in college teaching: Part II. *Education Media and Technology Yearbook* 23:59-74.

Fifield, S., and R. Peifer. 1994. Enhancing lecture presentations in introductory biology with computer-based multimedia. *Journal of College Science Teaching* 23(4): 235-239.

Janda, K. 1992. Multimedia in political science: Sobering lessons from a teaching experiment. *Journal of Educational Media and Hypermedia* 1:341-354.

Jensen, M. S., K. J. Wilcox, J. T. Hatch, and C. Somdahl. 1995. A computer-assisted instruction unit on diffusion and osmosis with a conceptual change design. *Journal of Computers in Mathematics and Science Teaching* 15(1/2): 49-64.

Leonard, W. H. 1992. A comparison of student performance following instruction by interactive video disc versus conventional laboratory. *Journal of Research in Science Teaching* 29:93-102.

Nantz, K. S., and F. Lundgren. 1998. Lecturing with technology. *Journal of College Teaching* 46(2): 53-56.

Palmiter, J. R. 1991. Effects of computer algebra systems on concept and skill acquisition in calculus. *Journal of Research in Mathematics in Education* 22:151-156.

Pearson, M., J. Folske, D. Paulson, and C. Burggraf. 1994. The relationship between student perceptions of the multimedia classroom and student perceptions of the multimedia classroom and student learning styles. Paper presented at the Eastern Communication Association Conference. Washington, D.C., May 1, 1994.

Privateer, P. M. 1999. Academic Technology and the future of higher education. *Journal of Higher Education* 70 (1): 60-79.

Spencer, K. 1991. Modes, media and methods: Search for educational effectiveness. *British Journal of Educational Effectiveness* 22:12-22.

Williamson, V. M., and M. R. Abraham. 1995. Effects of computer animation on the particulate mental models of college chemistry students. *Journal of Research in Science Teaching* 32: 521-534.

APPENDIX

SURVEY IN GLG 110-C LECTURE SECTION(S)

1. Classroom presentations of course materials in a format such as PowerPoint is <u>more interesting</u> than presentations of material in the more traditional lecture formats.

2. I feel it was easier for me to learn the presented material in the PowerPoint format than if the same were presented in the more traditional formats.

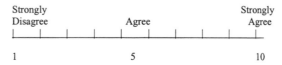

3. Class notes for a course available on the Internet is more desirable than the same available from other sources such as the reserved section at the library.

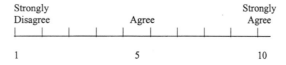

4. I feel it was easier for me to learn the presented materials in the classroom when class notes were available.

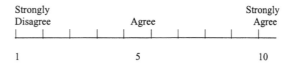

5. I feel the use of PowerPoint in the lectures and availability of Internet class notes <u>improved the overall learning</u> environment.

6. I feel Internet classnotes have been more important to me for learning the GLG 110 concepts than PowerPoint lecture slides used in the classroom.

Creating
Direct Channels
of Communication

Fostering Interaction with E-mail and In-class Notes

Gili Marbach-Ad and Phillip Sokolove

Biology students in a large-class, active-learning environment used e-mail and in-class written notes for student-instructor communication. Most students sent e-mail messages and about half were content-related. Messages from females and males reflected class gender distribution. Results also showed that African Americans were more likely to send content-related messages than other racial/ethnic groups.

What better way for students to broaden their learning than to ask questions or engage in dialogue? For over a decade, educators have drawn attention to the importance of students' questions and discussions in the teaching/learning process (Commeyras 1995; Dillon 1988; Good et al.1987). Even when teachers encourage questions, however, students—particularly those in large classes—are often reluctant to raise their hands to ask a question or to volunteer a comment. Consequently, in-class participation soon becomes limited to only a few individuals (Hedges and Mania-Farnell 1999).

One of the authors (PS) teaches a large, introductory biology course for majors that enrolls about 250 students. To encourage students to participate in class and to promote student-instructor and student-student interactions, he started in 1995 to teach this course em-

Gili Marbach-Ad was a postdoctoral research associate who is now a lecturer at Tel-Aviv University, and Phillip G. Sokolove is a professor, department of biological sciences, University of Maryland Baltimore County, 1000 Hilltop Circle, Baltimore, MD 21250; e-mail: gilim@post.tau.ac.il and sokolove@umbc.edu.

ploying student-centered, constructivist-based, and interactive instructional approaches (see Sokolove 1998). One example of his effort to build an interactive atmosphere in the classroom involved student name badges. Students were provided with pin-on name badges at the beginning of the semester and were required to wear them to every class session. Name badges enabled the instructor to become familiar with students' names (he could recall about half of them by the end of the semester) and allowed students (who were mainly freshmen) to get to know each other.

In this environment, frequent in-class questioning was strongly encouraged. Many students remained reluctant to participate in class, however, either because they were unsure of themselves or because of their temperament, their relative inexperience (first-semester freshmen), or their fear of embarrassment from peer reaction. One student in our class wrote: "When students ask overcomplicated or technical questions, peers 'eat them alive'."

Fostering Communication

To promote students' questions we concluded we would have to provide a "private channel" that would produce a secure and unthreatening environment for

student-instructor communication. Strauss and Fulwiler (1987, 1989) have advocated in-class writing as a means of communication between students and faculty. In a large college chemistry class they suggested that students write notes to the instructor about problems encountered in interpretation of material in the text and in lecture. A simple question box at the back of a large lecture room encouraged many students to put their concerns and confusion on paper (Strauss and Fulwiler 1987).

In our large, active-learning biology class all students were asked at the

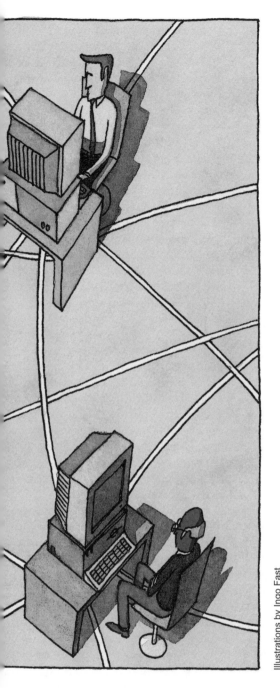

Illustrations by Ingo Fast

at the end of class in a special box for the instructor. During class sessions, lab notebooks were immediately accessible for those times when the instructor asked students to use them in individual exercises such as one-minute essays or for group problem solving. The lab notebook was always part of a student's in-class learning tools and was always within reach.

Another way to promote student communication with the instructor is through computer telecommunication. E-mail and other telecommunications methods (such as listservs, newsgroups, and computer conferencing) have been used by a number of college and university educators to improve interactions among students and between students and faculty in nonscience and science classes.

D'Souza (1992) evaluated the use of e-mail as a communication support aid in a lower-division business information systems course and reported that e-mail proved to be ideal for ensuring clear communication between the instructor and students and to meet specific learning needs. Many students in her study used e-mail to ask for special help or additional information on class lectures and out-of-class assignments.

Coombs (1992) used electronic mail and computer conferencing systems (electronic bulletin board) in an off-campus American history telecourse and reported that students recognized they were interacting via the computer differently than they might have in a classroom. They felt that they could express their feelings in a relatively anonymous way. Schoenfeld (1993) has also described the use of an electronic forum that provided a voice to every "anonymous" student.

Cavalier (1992) reported using an electronic bulletin board in an on-campus philosophy course in which the con-

venience of the system resulted in round-the-clock dialogues. Slovacek and Doyle-Nichols (1991), in their study on the use of electronic bulletin boards in college classes, suggested that asynchronous telecommunication allowed students and faculty to formulate messages ahead of time and therefore produce clearer, better-prepared questions and answers. Zack (1995) also reported using electronic messaging to improve the quality of instruction.

More recently Collins (1998) and Hedges and Mania-Farnell (1999) have used e-mail to improve communication in their introductory science classrooms (chemistry and biology). Hedges and Mania-Farnell reported that working with students via e-mail increased student-instructor interaction, helped students feel more comfortable about asking questions, and provided an opportunity to address individual problems. Collins, after using an electronic bulletin board, related that students' responses to an end-of-semester questionnaire suggested that even those who do not normally ask questions in large or small classes may do so through e-mail.

We, too, have employed electronic bulletin boards and newsgroups, but the majority of students in the class seem to view such forums in much the same way as the large lecture hall: they are too public, too "exposed," and (potentially) too embarrassing. Therefore, we decided to use unstructured e-mail to keep communication simple—and private—for both the students and us. E-mail is also convenient for students to use. Every student who matriculates at the University of Maryland Baltimore County (UMBC) is provided with a personal e-mail account, and many public computers (about 850) are available around the campus in various locations. In addition, there are approximately 1,500 computers in dorm rooms connected to the Internet. A significant number of students at this largely commuter campus also have access to e-mail on their home computers.

E-mail and Notebook Communication

This study was conducted in the introductory biology class offered in the fall of 1998. The instructor (PS) encouraged students to send him e-mail or in-class,

beginning of the semester to bring a chemistry laboratory notebook to each class session. The advantage of chemistry lab notebooks is that students can write a question or comment about a class topic or exercise to hand in to the instructor and still retain a copy for themselves (older chemistry lab notebooks had carbon paper between two pages so that the top page could be handed in for grading while the student retained the bottom page; modern notebooks use NCR paper to make the copy). Students were encouraged to write notes during class and leave them

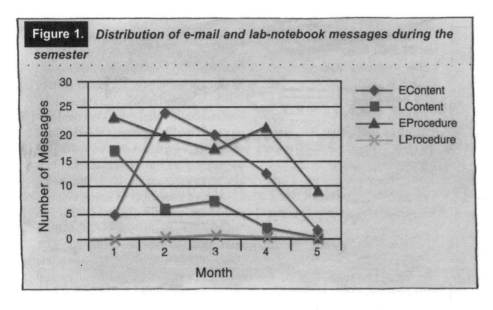

Figure 1. *Distribution of e-mail and lab-notebook messages during the semester*

Figure 2. *E-mail and lab notebook content-related messages by topic.*

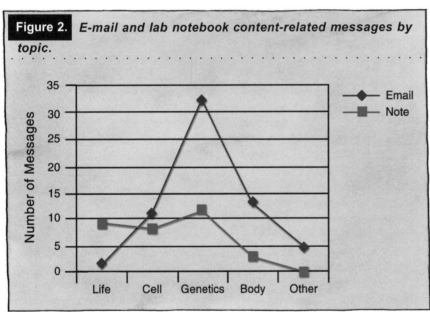

written, lab-notebook notes about anything they were interested in communicating (e.g., questions, comments, suggestions, complaints, etc.). At the end of the semester we examined all archived e-mail and lab-notebook notes that had been received along with all of the replies that the instructor had sent back to the students.

Over the course of the semester, 67 students in the class sent 150 e-mail messages and 33 written notes. Students' messages fell mainly into two categories: questions or comments about class content (63 e-mail messages and/or 32 written notes were received from 42 students) or procedural questions (87 e-mail messages from 38 students, and 1 written note).

Content-Related Messages

Content-related messages contained mainly questions about a topic that had been recently discussed in class. The number of content-related e-mail messages increased in the second month of the semester and decreased thereafter, while the number of written notes was highest at the beginning and decreased as the semester proceeded (fig. 1). Inspection of the data showed that eight of the students who wrote notes toward the beginning of the semester later switched to e-mail. It is difficult to identify the reason for the peak in content-related messages that occurred in the second month of the semester (fig 1). It might have been because that month the topics being covered were

genetics and evolution, which contain difficult concepts for many students. Indeed, about half of all content questions (32 e-mail messages and 12 written notes) dealt specifically with these topics (fig. 2). For example, one student asked: "If a [female] horse and a [male] donkey mate, a mule [is produced. But] the mule is not able to reproduce. . . . Is the mule considered to be a member of a species?"

Fewer questions dealt with the earlier topic of cell energetics (11 e-mail messages; 8 written notes). One student asked: "I understand how ATP is made. I even know what it is used for. What I would like to know is how ATP is used to carry out the necessary functions [of a cell]?" Other questions dealt with body systems (13 e-mail messages and 3 written notes): "What does the appendix actually do in animals that actually use it?" Some messages, mainly written notes, dealt with the first topic taught in the semester, "What is life?" (2 e-mail messages and 9 written notes): "When the virus connects to a host cell, doesn't it symbiotically become 'alive'?"

An immediate benefit derived from content-related messages is that some students will reflect a common misconception that can then be addressed in class. For example, learning about genetics and evolution, one student asked: "Can environmentally [induced] deformities become inherited deformities?" This is a common misconception in biology (Deadman and Kelly 1978; Engel, Clough, and Wood-Robinson 1985a, 1985b) that reflects students' acceptance of Lamarck's model for evolutionary change. In the next class session the instructor discussed the absurdity of the Lamarckian model: If true, this model would predict, for example, that the first child born to a skinny woman would be skinny too, but if she gained weight before her second child, the second child would be fat.

Another example of a misconception was raised by a student's e-mail message: "Since the NADH produced in glycolysis is later used in the electron transport system, does it also count as an intermediate?" This question shows that students sometimes have difficulty understanding that the same substance can be both an intermediate in a reaction and also a product (see Fisher 1985). The instructor's response, by e-mail, was: "A 'thing' can have two or more qualitative aspects at once. For example, you can be a U.S. citizen and at the same time be a Roman Catholic or Jewish (or whatever). NADH is, indeed, a product of glycolysis, and also an 'intermediate' in the overall process of aerobic respiration."

Some content-related questions are thoughtful and insightful: "Darwin's theory of evolution suggests that the environment keeps the number of reproducing individuals in check so that there is no overpopulation of a single species. Does this statement apply to the human population, too? [Or] are we an exception to this rule?" Others raise philosophical issues: "I was wondering, an offspring gets his traits from his parents. So what if his two parents were murderers or . . . criminals, and they always thought of doing harm to others. Is it true that their child would also be like them? And if that is true, don't you think it's unfair for them, as they will probably go to prison or get executed?"

Students write about events that they see or hear about or experience personally outside of the class that connect in some way to an in-class topic: "This got me to thinking about a summer science camp I went to the summer after my freshman year in high school. It was a gene cloning camp where we took bacteria that was sensitive to both kanamycin and ampicillin and made it resistant to both by using two other strains of bacteria, one resistant to the kanamycin and the other resistant to the ampicillin. . . . I saved my notes from that [summer,] and I can bring them with me to class if you would like."

The instructor was generally able to reply to students' e-mail messages or written notes within one or two days. Different answers were offered depending on the type of question a student asked. In many cases the instructor provided a short answer and referred the student to other sources of information (e.g., textbook, journal articles, or other instructors in the de-

Like e-mail, the lab notebook provides a channel of communication to the instructor that allows him or her to respond thoughtfully and yet rapidly to student queries. Unlike e-mail, however, lab notebooks never crash.

partment). In some cases the instructor recommended that the student work with his or her cooperative group to find an answer or try to raise the question in his or her discussion section. One student wrote to the instructor after receiving such a recommendation: "Thanks for the advice about forming a 'Chemiosmosis' group. I arranged a meeting with my [cooperative] group and we all went over the concept. I now understand it much better. . . ."

In a number of cases the instructor wrote a longer answer (such replies could exceed 500-1000 words), and in yet other cases he challenged the student to research the topic and bring the information gathered back to the class. For example, the instructor wrote to a student who had asked about enzyme pills, "How about finding out for us how those enzyme pills work?" Two days later the student sent him the following message: "After an extensive internet search, I ended up with a phone number for the makers of the Lactaid pill. They told me that the active ingredient in the pills is actually the lactase enzyme itself. How they get the enzyme into the pill is unclear to me. However they said they would send me a packet on lactose intolerance along with a free sample of the product. I believe this is a credible source of information because the producers of Lactaid are also the producers of several other drugs such as Tylonol and Nasalcrom (a nasal spray for allergy symptoms)."

Procedural Messages

Almost all of the procedural messages

were sent by e-mail: 57 percent included questions on take-home assignments (how to cite references, how many pages to write, and where to find information sources) and questions about exams or exam scores; 10 percent reported that the student would be absent from class; eight percent requested a change in discussion section or lecture class; and 11 percent (received mainly toward the end of the semester) were about how the student felt in this innovative class (some of these even thanked the instructor). A few students complained about their teammates or about their graduate teaching assistant (TA). The frequency of procedural messages was roughly constant over the course of the semester (fig. 1). About 20 messages were received each month.

Who Is Likely to Communicate?

Table 1 compares the demographic distribution of students who sent content-related e-mail messages or written notes and the demographic distribution of the entire class. About half of the students who sent e-mail messages were majoring in biology or in biochemistry (even though only a third of the students in the class were majoring in these areas), while the other half were majoring in other areas or were undecided.

Two-thirds of the students who sent content-related messages were female, which roughly reflected the percentage of women in the class. In contrast, the percentage of students sending content-related messages who were African American (24 percent) was much greater than their total percentage in the class (14 percent), while among Caucasians the relationship was reversed (48 percent of those who sent content-related messages were Caucasians vs. 60 percent in the entire class). This was interesting in light of the fact that in another study (Sokolove and Marbach-Ad 1999) we found African American students were more likely than Caucasians or other racial/ethnic groups to study with others for exams. Treisman (1992) suggests that African American students who are accepted to good universities are highly motivated and prepared to comply with an instructor's suggestions to succeed. In the active-learning class, the instructor urged students to communicate with him and to study with

Table 1. *Demographic distribution of students who sent content-related messages relative to their distribution in the whole class.*

	Percent of students who sent content-related messages*	Percent of students in class**
Primary Major		
Biology or Biochemistry	50	32
Other and undecided	50	68
Gender		
Female	67	60
Male	33	40
Race/Ethnicity		
Caucasian	48	60
Asian	26	25
African American	24	14
Other	2	1
Final grade in class		
A	52	21
B	29	31
C	17	33
D	0	10
F	2	5

*N=42
**The total number of students in class=249

others in order to get better scores. It seems that the African Americans in this class were more likely than other groups to follow these recommendations. Also, in this class a larger proportion of African American students were biology or biochemistry majors (45 percent) than were Caucasians (34 percent), and biology/biochemistry majors tended to contribute more content-related messages (table 1).

We also found a strong correlation between the number of students who sent content-related messages and final grades: 52 percent of the students who sent content-related messages earned As, while only 21 percent of the entire class earned an A as the final grade.

The use of e-mail to communicate with an instructor outside of normal class time has been previously linked to improved academic performance (Slovacek and Doyle-Nichols 1991). However, the fact that students with higher grades were more likely to send messages than

those with lower grades might indicate either that student-instructor communication enhanced student achievement or simply that good students have a tendency to send more e-mail messages and/or written notes to the instructor. Our data do not allow us to distinguish between these alternatives.

Final Thoughts
Our observations and informal student feedback suggest that both e-mail messages and written notes provide important tools for student-instructor communication, particularly for students who can not wait around after class or who are hesitant (or unable) to find time to schedule an office appointment to meet privately with the instructor. Students have noted that around-the-clock availability of the system allows them to ask questions and receive answers at any time of day or night. From the instructor's point of view, the system encourages

more frequent student-instructor interaction and allows students to "find" him without having to track him down or to schedule a face-to-face meeting. He, in turn, can answer students' questions and respond to their requests in his free time.

We believe that in combination these two modes of communication support and enhance an active-learning environment. They allow instructors to offer more personalized attention to students in meeting their specific learning needs, and they provide an opportunity for students to ask for special help or for additional information about class lectures and out-of-class assignments. The act of writing is also a good way to clarify ideas and understanding (Laurillard 1999). The use of e-mail allows students and instructors to compose messages in advance, thus producing clearer, better-prepared questions and answers.

E-mail, however, is of little use when a student has a question in class and is either too shy or intimidated or embarrassed to speak out. The advantage of using lab notebooks is that students can write to the instructor with a sense of immediacy as well as privacy. Although handwritten notes are sometimes difficult to read and often phrased poorly, such notes are extraordinarily helpful, since they represent the student's spontaneous thoughts and understandings concerning in-class events and discussions. All too often, the student who waits to send his or her thoughts via an out-of-class computer does so rarely, if at all. Like e-mail, the lab notebook provides a channel of communication to the instructor that allows him or her to respond thoughtfully and yet rapidly to student queries. Unlike e-mail, however, lab notebooks never crash.

Note
Research supported in part by a grant from the National Science Foundation, REC-9815007. Any opinions, findings, and conclusions or recommendations expressed in this publication are those of the authors and do not necessarily reflect the views of the National Science Foundation.

References

Cavalier, R.J. 1992. Course processing and redesigning. *Educom Review* 27:32-37.

Collins, M.A.J. 1998. Using electronic bulletin boards with college biology classes. *The American Biology Teacher* 57:188-189.

Commeyras, M. 1995. What can we learn from students' questions? *Theory into Practice* 34(2): 101-106.

Coombs, N. 1992. Teaching in the information age. *Educom Review* 27:28-31.

Deadman, J.A., and P.J. Kelly. 1978. What do secondary school boys understand about evolution and heredity before they are taught the topics? *Journal of Biological Education* 12(1): 7-15.

Dillon, J.T. 1988. The remedial status of student questioning. *Journal of Curriculum Studies* 20(3): 197-210.

D'Souza, P.V. 1992. E-mail's role in the learning process: A case study. *Journal of Research on Computing in Education* 25:254-264.

Engel Clough, E., and C. Wood-Robinson. 1985a. How secondary students inherent instances of biological adaptation. *Journal of Biological Education* 19(2): 125-129.

Engel Clough, E., and C. Wood-Robinson. 1985b. Children's understanding of inheritance. *Journal of Biological Education* 19(4): 304-310.

Fisher, K.M. 1983. A misconception in biology: Amino acids and translation. *Journal of Research in Science Teaching* 22: 53–62

Good, T.L., R.L. Slavings, K. H. Harel, and H. Emerson. 1987. Student passivity: A study of question asking in K-12 classrooms. *Sociology of Education* 60:181-199.

Hedges, K., and B. Mania-Farnell. 1999. Using E-mail to improve communication in the introductory science classroom. *Journal of College Science Teaching* 28:198-202.

Laurillard, D. 1999. Using communications and information technology effectively. In *Teaching Tips: Strategies, Research, and Theory for College and University Teachers,* ed. W.J. McKeeachie, 183-200. New York: Houghton Mifflin.

Schoenfeld, C. 1993. Electronic forum vivifies the classroom. *Academic Leader* 9:1.

Slovacek S.P., and A.R. Doyle-Nichols. 1991. Enhancing telecommunication in teacher education. *Journal of Research on Computing in Education* 24: 254-264.

Sokolove, P.G. 1998. The challenge of teaching Biology 100: Can I really promote active learning in a large lecture? In *Journeys of Transformation*, eds. M.B. Gardner and D.L. Ayres, 121-128. College Park, MD: Maryland Collaborative for Teacher Preparation.

Sokolove, P.G, and G. Marbach-Ad. 1999. The benefits of out-of-group study for improving student performance on exams: A comparison of outcomes in active learning and traditional college biology classes. *Journal on Excellence in College Teaching* 10: 49–68.

Strauss, M., and T. Fulwiler. 1987. Interactive writing and learning chemistry. *Journal of College Science Teaching* 16:256-262.

Strauss, M., and T. Fulwiler. 1989. Writing to learn in large classes. *Journal of College Science Teaching* 19:158-163.

Treisman, U. 1992. Studying students studying calculus: A look at the lives of minority mathematics students in college. *The College Mathematics Journal* 23:362-372.

Zack, M.H. 1995. Using electronic messaging to improve the quality of instruction. *Journal of Education for Business* 70:202-206.

Using Action Research to Bring the Large Class Down to Size

Employing Focused Classroom Investigations to Improve Individual Teaching Practices

Jeffrey P. Adams and Timothy F. Slater

Particularly at the college level, a truism exists that the professors who are most closely involved in the day-to-day process of science teaching are often unfamiliar with the corresponding educational research base. Many research scientists recognize that their classroom instruction needs improvement yet they discover that the traditional educational research literature often fails to provide insight of immediate utility.

In 1986, Hustler, Cassidy, and Cuff went so far as to suggest that nearly everyone with a direct interest in classroom teaching is disenchanted with traditional educational research because it appears to be irrelevant and impractical to the real classroom. An alternative paradigm that seeks to bridge the gap between research and teaching and provide a new model for professional practice is *action research*.

After briefly reviewing the history of the action research movement, this article summarizes several action research studies recently conducted at Montana State University in an introductory astronomy course. These results are not presented as having generalizable implications but rather as examples of how to include systematic inquiry as an integral part of the teaching process.

WHAT IS ACTION RESEARCH?

An enormous amount of what constitutes successful instruction gets passed informally from experienced faculty members to newer faculty members. This is because informal success and failure stories address specific classroom situations and are expressed in the language of faculty.

Most faculty cannot afford the time or expense to use highly validated cognitive instruments, control groups, psychometric item response analysis, or other hallmarks of traditional educational research to determine exactly which individual instructional activities are working or not working in their classrooms. Further, when faculty discuss teaching with colleagues, it is in the common language of their profession and not in the highly specialized language of the educational researcher. (For example, Factor Analysis makes a lot more sense to scientists when described as an Eigenvalue problem.)

Action research respects this informal tradition of reflective practice (Schön 1983) and provides a framework for faculty-led inquiry and dissemination aimed specifically at enhancing the learning environment.

In general, there are six key questions that provide the structure of action research methods and results. These questions can be abbreviated as: what did the pupils actually do; what were they learning; how worthwhile was it; what did the teacher/researcher do; what did the teacher/researcher learn; and what will the teacher/researcher do now? One of several excellent resources for suggestions on how to address these questions is *Classroom Assessment Techniques* by Angelo and Cross (1993).

The term "action research" was coined in 1947 by Kurt Lewin during a problem-driven effort to conduct sociology research aimed specifically at enacting changes in social programs (McKernan 1991). As Lewin saw it,

Jeffrey P. Adams is an assistant professor of physics at Montana State University, Bozeman, MT 59717; e-mail: adams@physics.montana.edu. Timothy F. Slater is a research assistant professor of physics and the lead project science director for the Montana NASA Center for Educational Resources (CERES) Project at Montana State University, P.O. Box 170560, Bozeman, MT 59717-0560; e-mail: tslater@physics.montana.edu.

the role of the researcher was both to promote and understand the process of change and as such could not be treated as distinct from the system under study.

This paradigm, which rejected the notion of researcher as disconnected observer, was not new to education theorists but it did provide an added impetus to the teacher-as-researcher movement. As applied to the study of education, the action research concept recognized the central role of the teacher as both the primary agent of change in the classroom and the one best able to interpret the results.

Readers interested in tracing the rich history of action research, which goes back more than fifty years, as well as the surrounding philosophical foundations, are urged to consult Carr and Kemmis (1986) and Hustler, Cassidy, and Cuff (1986) and references therein.

The two primary characteristics of action research that separate it from traditional lines of educational inquiry are that it is conducted by active participants in the teaching/learning process and that it is expressed in the language of its practitioners. Action research has been aggressively promoted in the K-12 arena as providing a model for the professionalization of teachers in which teachers become the primary focus of their own professional development. The goal is to encourage teachers to systematically study the impact of making change within their own classrooms.

At the college and university level, action research provides a mechanism for transforming the role of faculty from that of researchers who occasionally lecture to a perspective that recognizes teaching as a scholarly creative activity (Boyer 1990; Rice 1996).

The environment and natural language of college and university science instructors is clearly not the same as for most K-12 teachers. Whereas teachers are likely put off by extended discussions of experimental method-

Kurt Lewin (1890-1947), a social psychologist and former director of the Group Dynamics Research Center at M.I.T., coined the term "action research" in 1947.

CORBIS-BETTMANN

ologies, control groups, sampling procedures, and data analysis, these terms and approaches comprise the natural language of research scientists—often a very different language than that used by some of our colleagues in colleges of education.

SOME ACTION RESEARCH RESULTS

Briefly summarized, here are four action research studies conducted at Montana State University in support of improving introductory astronomy, a course with an enrollment of more than 200 nonscience major undergraduates in a single lecture. These methods and results are meant to be brief examples of how we have used action research to learn more about our classroom and positively impact students. More detailed methods and results are available by contacting the authors.

Question #1: Can we quickly determine students' precourse knowledge without using an extensive pretest? This is important for modifying the pace of instruction and creating effective col-

laborative working groups.

The approach was to survey students to find out how they rated their level of understanding of seven specific astronomy concepts both before and after instruction (pretest/posttest strategy). The results were then matched to student performance on a 21-item multiple-choice test. Sample self-report and corresponding multiple-choice items are shown in **Figure 1**.

Comparing pretest to posttest gains we found: (1) there were statistically significant student gains on students' self-report of knowledge ($self_{pre}$=2.36 to $self_{post}$=3.71 on a scale of 1 to 5) implying that the 5-level self-report survey is sensitive enough to measure perceived gains in knowledge; (2) there were significant student gains on multiple-choice items (MC_{pre}=50% to MC_{post}=70%) implying that learning did occur; (3) there was a reasonably high correlation between self-report and exam performance (r_{pre}=.46 and r_{post}=.39 where r=0 is no correlation and r=1 is perfect correlation); and (4) males self-report slightly higher than females, but demonstrate no difference in performance.

This analysis suggests that self-report gains are representative of actual student gains on multiple-choice scores and that students can accurately recognize and accurately report their knowledge levels. It appears that, within the context of this class, two-minute self-report surveys can be substituted for conventional 20-minute pretest exams to estimate students' initial knowledge state.

Question #2: Does required e-mail contact between students and faculty improve instructor availability ratings on faculty evaluation forms?

The approach was to award points to students for e-mailing the instructor twice during the semester. The students were encouraged to use the opportunity to initiate a meaningful interaction but understood that points were awarded irrespective of the content of the message—the instructor recorded in a personal journal the perceived meaningfulness of each electronic interaction. The instructor replied to all messages and, where e-mail was not the appropriate medium to hold the discussion, followed up with a phone call.

In the semester prior to implementing this strategy, the instructor received 15 e-mail messages from students and received an instructor availability rating of $\underline{x}$ =1.83 (1 (*good*) to 5 (*poor*)). With the new strategy in place, the instructor received 157 e-mail messages; 149 of which were judged to be meaningful. In addition, many students, who likely would not have done so without some encouragement, continued to e-mail the instructor. Surprising, however, the overall rating of instructor availability remained essentially constant at 1.88. These results suggest that student ratings of instructor availability are not impacted by e-mail communication even though the instructor's perception was an overall increase in meaningful interactions with students.

Question #3: *How do student writing skills correlate with exam performance?*

Students in this course are required to complete three one-page writing assignments, each graded for content, grammar, and style. The assigned topics are not highly technical and encourage creativity. For example: "Since the time of Copernicus, we have known that the earth circles the sun and yet newspapers still report the times that the sun rises and sets, suggesting that the sun rotates around the earth. Is it wrong to use a model that is inherently flawed?"

This task is very different than the homework and exams, which focus much more on technical knowledge. We were interested in how well student performance on the writing task was related to their performance on the multiple-choice exams.

We examined the correlation between each student's final exam score and her/his average writing score. A scatter plot of the data is shown in **Figure 2**. A correlation analysis, easily performed on most spreadsheet programs, yielded a correlation coefficient of r=0.50. To get a better sense of the meaning of this number, we compared students' final exams scores with their scores on chapter tests and weekly homework. The correlation with the chapter tests was higher at 0.76, as one would expect. Surprisingly though, the correlation between final exam scores and homework scores was only 0.45, which is slightly lower than the correlation with writing assignments.

The data contradicted our initial hypothesis that, based on content similarity, the final exam scores would be more highly correlated to the homework than the writing assignments. This suggests a more integral connection between writing and test performance than we had anticipated—a connection that must be recognized in any future course revisions.

Question #4: *What is working well and not so well in implementing collaborative learning groups in the large lecture course?*

In the fall of 1997, we made major course revisions to our astronomy class.

Figure 1. Example of Self-Report and Corresponding Multiple Choice Questions

<u>Self-Report Question:</u>

Listed below are major concepts in astronomy. For each concept, rate your current level of understanding using the scale below.

Score 1 - I have never heard of this concept before.

Score 2 - I have heard of this before but I don't understand it.

Score 3 - I think I understand this concept.

Score 4 - I understand this concept well.

Score 5 - I understand this concept completely.

{*never heard of it* $\Leftarrow$ 1 2 3 4 5 $\Rightarrow$ *understand completely*}

(circle one)

5. how we know that Venus orbits the Sun   1 2 3 4 5

<u>Corresponding Multiple Choice Questions</u>

1. In what direction would you have to look to see Venus just after sunset?
a. north
b. south
c. east
d. west*

13. Galileo concluded that Venus orbits the Sun because
a. Venus demonstrates phases like the moon.*
b. he saw it move with his telescope.
c. of the Pisa Tower experiment.
d. ancient myths predicted it.

21. Venus is observed in full phase (i.e., appears as a fully lit disc). Which of the following statements is true?
a. Venus is about as close to Earth as possible (near side of orbit).
b. Venus appears about as far from the Sun as possible (i.e., it is separated from the Sun by a large angle).
c. Venus is about as far from Earth as possible (far side of orbit).*

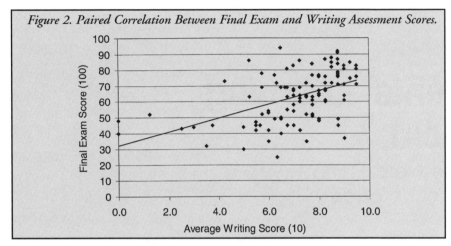

Figure 2. Paired Correlation Between Final Exam and Writing Assessment Scores.

The goal was to increase student participation and attendance by incorporating frequent small group discussion activities into the lecture environment. We developed a series of 16 mini-labs for students to complete working in groups of four. Each activity required between 20 and 50 minutes to finish with each student receiving the group score. Both quizzes and examinations contained a group component.

To evaluate the implementation of this innovative approach, we coerced 10 faculty from across campus to audiotape exploratory focus group discussions with groups of up to 20 students. A survey of 10 hours of audiotape revealed the following: students enjoy the alternation between activity and lecture; students report learning from each other; students would prefer to have a more detailed reading list than was initially provided; the structure of the exam needed to be more clearly defined; and students would like to have more specific roles and responsibilities in their collaborative learning groups.

The results of these interviews were reported to the class as a whole and, where feasible, changes were implemented to address students' concerns. End of course surveys indicated that some of the students' concerns were addressed by our mid-course corrections and that the students appreciated the process. Students informally commented that this experience demonstrated that the instructors cared about students' learning.

DISCUSSION

It is our thesis that the college learning environment can be substantially improved by making decisions based on data. As scientists, we have powerful analysis skills that can inform and improve the classroom environment when directed at the issues of teaching and learning.

As demonstrated by the above examples, focused classroom investigations can provide insights not available through casual observation. These insights can then direct curricular or instructional practices toward achieving the ultimate goal of improved student learning—a process called action research. Rather than focusing on generalizability as a means of adding to the educational literature base, action research provides a paradigm for both documenting our efforts to improve our classes *and* communicating successes and failures to our peers, thus elevating teaching to a scholarly activity (Boyer 1990; Rice 1996).

Moreover, by including observations of student behavior and student attitude surveys in addition to measures of student achievement, we have gained substantial insight into what our students expect. Probably the most exciting aspect is that not only is our instruction improving, but also students appreciate having their perspectives acknowledged as partners in the learning process—a partnership that carries with it both rights and responsibilities.

Finally, we live in a time when, aside from the personal desire of professors to see their students learn as effectively as possible, there is increasing external pressure to demonstrate competence in teaching to stakeholders in education. Action research is an approach to teaching that simultaneously leads to the improvement of instructional practices (Angelo 1991) and the creation of products that comprise a teaching portfolio to be used by faculty and administration as tangible evidence of teaching success.

As colleges and universities are beginning to place more emphasis on effective teaching, action research methods and results provide a recognized structure for demonstrating reflective practice. ∎

References
Anderson, Elaine J. 1997. Active learning in the lecture hall. *Journal of CollegeScience Teaching* 26(6): 428-429.
Angelo, Thomas K. 1991. *Classroom Research: Early Lessons from Success.* San Francisco: Jossey-Bass.
Angelo, Thomas, and K. Patricia Cross. 1993. *Classroom Assessment Techniques: A Handbook for College Teachers.* 2nd ed. San Francisco: Jossey-Bass.
Bonwell, Charles C., and James A. Eison. 1991. *Active Learning: Creating Excitement in the Classroom.* ASHE-ERIC Higher Education Report No. 1. Washington D.C.: The George Washington University, School of Education and Human Development.
Boyer, E. 1990. *Scholarship Reconsidered: Priorities of the Professoriate.* Princeton: The Carnegie Foundation.
Carr, Wilfred, and Stephen Kemmis. 1986. *Becoming Critical: Education, Knowledge, and Action Research.* Philadelphia: Falmer Press.
Cross, K. Patricia. 1990. Classroom research: Helping professors learn more about teaching and learning. In *How Administrators Can Improve Teaching: Moving from Talk to Action in Higher Education*, ed. P. Seldin and Associates. San Francisco: Jossey-Bass.
Hustler, Cassidy, and Cuff. 1986. *Action Research in Classrooms and Schools.* Allen & Unwin: Boston.
McKernan, J. 1991. *Curriculum Action Research: A Handbook of Methods and Resources for the Reflective Practitioner.* New York: St. Martin's Press.
Rice, R. Eugene. 1996. *Making a Place for the New American Scholar.* Washington DC: American Association for Higher Education.
Schön, Donald A. 1983. *The Reflective Practitioner: How Professionals Think in Action.* United States: Harper Collins.

Gauging Students' Learning in the Classroom

An Assessment Tool to Help Refine Instructors' Teaching Techniques

Judith E. Heady

To find out what helps students to learn, the author administered Elaine Seymour's Student Assessment of Learning Gains instrument to her introductory biology classes. Using the student feedback from the 1998 semester, she changed her teaching the following year. As a result, students' numerical responses to several learning gains increased.

In the face of reports that students are not learning science effectively (Kyle 1997; Lord 1999; Schmidt and McKnight 1998), I wanted to know what actually helps them to learn. How could I find out? Would tests and grades tell me? What about traditional student evaluations of the material?

Instead of blindly experimenting with innovations that might or might not be beneficial, I decided to go straight to the source: the students themselves. Elaine Seymour and her colleagues (Wiese et al. 1999; Seymour et al. 2000) devised an instrument, Student Assessment of Learning Gains (SALG), that is a valid and reliable way to measure student learning. (This tool is available online at *http://www.wcer.wisc.edu/salgains/instructor*.) I used the instrument for two years as a guide to help me adjust my teaching and to improve my students' perceptions of their classroom experiences.

Judith E. Heady is an associate professor, department of natural sciences, University of Michigan-Dearborn, 4901 Evergreen Road, Dearborn, MI 48128; e-mail: jheady@umich.edu.

I expected that the student feedback on the SALG form would indicate whether or not the changes I instituted in my course were helpful to students. I realize that each class is unique and that what works for one group may not work for another. The questions asked, however, were sufficiently specific that some basic changes were likely to spark improvement (or reveal elements worthy of elimination).

Class Structure

Biology 130 (Introduction to Organismal and Environmental Biology) is one of two introductory courses for biology majors at the University of Michigan-Dearborn. The class, which enrolled 60 students in each of the fall semesters of 1998 and 1999, meets weekly for three one-hour classroom sessions and one four-hour period. In this latter period, 20 students meet in one of three sections for one hour of recitation-discussion and three hours of laboratory.

The classroom sessions include mini-lectures, discussions within groups of four students (assigned at the beginning of the term), group problem-solving exercises, group and individual quizzes, and informal group presentations. The classroom is conducive to group work, containing small tables and portable chairs. Students have daily framework-question sheets to guide their preparation for class and to help the groups solve the problems and do well on the quizzes. I keep a record of participation for all oral and written classroom activities. This score accounts for one-eighth of students' overall grades.

Recitation sessions are used to review topics, ask and answer questions, introduce new activities that support an important lecture concept, and present laboratory projects results. The laboratories consist of four three-week projects on the following course topic areas: ecology and the environment, genetics and evolution, plant anatomy and physiology, and animal anatomy and physiology. Assessment of these projects include oral presentations, written assignments, and general participation. Students provide peer and self-assessment of their individual and group activities according to directions and rubrics I distribute at the beginning of the term.

To compare fall 1998 and fall 1999 classes, I collected demographic data on the students (table 1). I did not find any significant differences between the two classes. The university offered the classroom sessions at the same times and in the same room both years. I gave the

Table 1. *Student demographics of Biology 130 classes.*

Student Information	Fall 1998	Fall 1999
Average ACT Score	23.1	24.0
H.S. Grade Point Average	3.3	3.4
Biology and Related Majors[1]	27/57	22/55
Preservice K-8 Teachers[2]	10/57	15/55
First-time Freshmen	28/57	20/55

[1] Biology, biochemistry, biology-track environmental science, and microbiology majors
[2] All of the K-8 preservice teachers were science majors or minors

Table 2. *Pre- and post-test results on student exams assessing knowledge gained.[1]*

Categories / Topics	1998		1999	
	Pre	Post	Pre	Post
Environmental/Ecology	14[2]	54	13	49
Genetics/Evolution	14	51	21	39
Classification	32	100	58	89
Plant Anatomy/Physiology	15	52	17	69
Animal Anatomy/Physiology	3	95	17	NA

[1] There were eight very similar questions on both pretests; post-test questions were generally part of the final examination.
[2] Each number represents the percent of students who answered the questions correctly. Those who answered the questions partially correctly were not included. The proportion of the students [both years] who answered each of the eight questions completely incorrectly on the pretest were nearly the same.

survey under similar circumstances each year. Results of 1998 and 1999 pre- and post-tests, similar to those I have given for several years, were not radically different from those of the previous years or from each other (table 2). These results again show that the two groups were similar in their initial knowledge base and in what they learned.

Administering the SALG Instrument

The SALG instrument uses a Likert scale ranked from low to high and features questions that stress student perception of gains in understanding and aspects of the course that promoted learning. The instrument form, which contains room for written responses, has five major question sections that each include several specific items. The form can also be tailored for any class, but the changes must still focus on what students feel helped them learn. This is not an evaluation of the instructor.

I downloaded the SALG form from the website listed above and handed it out to the students to complete. I also made the following modifications: I substituted "biology" for "chemistry," added information to explain why I included particular questions, and used course-specific activities or concepts in slots reserved for them. I retained all general questions and categories from the SALG instrument.

In 1998 and 1999 students had up to 25 minutes to take the SALG test anonymously near the end of the terms. I analyzed the results and used a two-tailed t-test in Quattro Pro 8 to compare the feedback from the two groups.

I did change my pedagogy in response to student feedback and after analyzing my teaching. Because I altered my teaching techniques, some of the questions were modified in 1999 and were not comparable to those used in 1998. In this paper I include only a few of the questions that I analyzed,

such as those that show significant change and those that I expected to alter the following year.

Results of the SALG Surveys

In the fall of 1998, I surveyed 52 of 57 students and in the fall of 1999, 49 of 55 students. In both 1998 and 1999 students' comments were varied, but comments were on similar topics and students provided similar numbers of positive and negative remarks. Responses to three comparable short-answer questions, however, were significantly different in 1999 (table 3). Answers to all three show aspects of learning were statistically different in a positive direction. Other responses moved to a more positive level but not significantly, including several subcategories of question 1: "discussions in class"; "opportunities for in-class review"; "quality of contact with the teacher"; and "the way that this class was taught overall."

Many responses stayed the same, including the subcategories "plant project laboratories" and "the text." Responses to questions 2 and 3 also remained the same: "animal structure and function" and "giving oral presentations." A few questions had lower numerical responses, but none were significant: "working with peers outside of class" (question 1) and "knowledge about a variety of information sources" (question 4). Table 4 provides a class mean for all of the student responses on the SALG instrument.

Comparison Between 1998 and 1999

What contributed to the changes in responses between 1998 and 1999? Several contributing factors might include high school classes that had more classroom activities and more group learning, different students who might have responded to the 1998 pedagogies similarly to the altered ones in 1999, other factors in the lives of these students that cannot be controlled, and the changes I made in my pedagogies. I cannot measure the first three factors, but with 60 students it is reasonable to suspect that these variables would not be likely to affect the outcome. The variable of interest is the change in my pedagogy in response to student feedback and to self-evaluation of my class.

I cannot readily explain the large numerical increase in "the pace at which we worked" (question 1), but, after analyzing my teaching, I tried to organize activities better and provide more detailed framework-question sheets and greater acceptance of the groups, which might have contributed to this feeling.

The most important change in student responses for me was the large increase in feeling that "group work in class" (question 1) helped students to learn. In 1999, I invited a sociology professor with expertise in group dynamics to share some information and experience with my students (Caprio et al. 1998). This professor, a consultant for industry and other for-profit busnesses,

discussed how important working as groups is to the commercial world and how that benefits each member of the group as well as the company.

Certainly the numerical increase in "understanding the main concepts" (question 4) is gratifying and might indicate that functioning groups helped students to gain greater understanding of the material. If the whole tenor of the class were improved and the pace more accepted, then the environment would likely support better knowledge acquisition. The more specific framework questions might have identified the important concepts to master. More students in 1999 recognized that the review sessions were helpful (question 1), and that might indicate that they discerned the important points to study.

Several course exercises yielded the same or very similar responses both years (table 3). I expected that to happen since I did not change those aspects of the course (and considering the classes were similar). Students completed the same plant and animal projects in the laboratory, and many of the classroom activities were the same. Oral presentation opportunities were nearly the same for both years, and I emphasized ways to make students feel more confident (e.g., by stressing the research process, not just research answers, and by underscoring group decision making over individual opinion) during the term equally both years. On other occasions where I did not change the course, only minor shifts in responses (e.g., in the "writing papers"

Table 3. Selected student responses on the SALG instrument.		
Question 1. How much did each of the following aspects of the class help your learning?	1998	1999
The pace at which we worked	2.42 ± 1.19[1]	3.04 ± 1.01[2]
The class and lab activities: discussions in class	2.76 ± 1.25	3.14 ± 1.03
The class and lab activities: group work in class	2.50 ± 1.25	3.00 ± 1.12[3]
The class and lab activities: treasure hunt (experiences)[4]	2.33 ± 1.28	2.57 ± 1.28
The class and lab activities: plant project laboratories	3.16 ± 1.21	3.16 ± 1.18
Tests, graded activities, and assignments: opportunities for in-class review	2.71 ± 1.40	3.11 ± 1.12
Resources: the text	3.60 ± 1.06	3.59 ± 1.03
Individual support as a learner: the quality of contact with the teacher (in class, extra sessions, 1:1 in office/e-mail)	3.23 ± 1.19	3.46 ± 1.31
Individual support as a learner: working with peers outside of class	3.32 ± 1.16	3.19 ± 1.23
The way that this class was taught overall	2.68 ± 1.24	3.00 ± 1.12
Question 2. As a result of your work in this class, how well do you think that you now understand the following?		
Animal structure and function	3.58 ± 0.93	3.59 ± 1.07
Question 3. How much has this class added to your skills in each of the following?		
Writing papers	2.10 ± 0.97	2.37 ± 1.00
Giving oral presentations	3.31 ± 1.07	3.31 ± 1.16
Question 4. To what extent did you make gains in any of the following as a result of what you did in this class?		
Understanding the main concepts	3.12 ± 0.95	3.51 ± 0.95[5]
Understanding the relationship between concepts	3.14 ± 0.98	3.49 ± 0.88
Knowledge about a variety of information sources	3.12 ± 1.05	2.90 ± 1.30

[1] Average of responses and standard deviation of the mean
[2] Significant to the =0.01 level; p = 0.003
[3] Significant to the =0.05 level; p = 0.039
[4] Aspects in parentheses were added in 1999; they did not substantially change the focus of the question so are included
[5] Significant to the =0.05 level; p = 0.042

Table 4.	Class means of student responses on the SALG instrument.[1]			
Year	Class Size	SALG Participants	Class Means	Standard Deviation
1998	57	52	3.03	0.41
1999	55	49	3.14	0.32

[1] 1998 started with 59 students; 1999 with 60 students. Students most often dropped because of lack of interest/desire to participate fully in a biology course for majors. All who dropped in both years were nonbiology majors; only one freshman was in the school of education. One student in 1999 had to drop because of illness.

category—question 3) indicate that these two classes were similar.

Even though no responses in 1999 were significantly lower than in 1998, several were marginally lower (table 3). I am only concerned with "working with peers outside of class" (question 1) and "information sources" (question 4). I expected that the group experiences in the classroom and laboratory would encourage students to work together outside of class. And the Treasure Hunt (Switzer and Yoder 1996), the use of research articles in the classroom, and the availability of many helpful Internet sites were intended to expose the students to non-textbook sources of information.

Did I try to change some other aspects of the course after 1998 and fail to see positive responses from students in 1999? I expected to see a more positive response to the Treasure Hunt (question 1) because I changed the 24-point portion from an animal behavior project to a comprehensive concept map. (I changed because most students did not understand how to do the exercise to achieve the lesson I was trying to teach.) Students responded favorably to the concept map when asked about it separately as: "How much did each of the following aspects of the class help your learning: concept map for Treasure Hunt" (3.04 ± 1.29).

There was a wide variation as might be expected, because some people find concept maps very useful and others do not, but this was an exercise that had more direct application to the final exam. Also, the Treasure Hunt allowed students to experience other sources of learning, such as attending guest lectures and participating in field trips.

Student written comments demonstrated the variability of attitudes toward the course and several common concerns. The areas most often mentioned as sources of concern were the groups, matching important concepts and examinations, and lack of understanding of what students should be doing. I have responded to and will continue to respond to these concerns. The expression of enjoyment and learning from most students, however, confirmed their approval of the course.

Comparisons with the Modular Chemistry Classes

Many of my survey questions cannot be compared with the chemistry classes studied by Elaine Seymour and her colleagues (Wiese et al. 1999; Seymour et al. 2000). Their class formats were not the same, and in biology "problem solving" does not mean the same thing as it does in chemistry. Nonetheless, I decided to look at my total class means in 1998 and 1999 (table 4) to see whether or not they fit into the range described for all of the classes at the institutions Seymour and her colleagues studied. My students' overall average response is lower than most from the smaller classes and is fairly close in size or higher than the large, research university classes. The items that received the lowest responses by my students were discontinued after 1998 or were dramatically altered in 2000. The variable number of questions used among the institutions probably means that such an overall comparison should be considered only very generally. The most important comparisons should come from individual items that are not too specific to the particular courses.

One of the goals of my classes included gaining comfort in "giving oral presentations" (question 3). The responses on that skill were below average for Seymour's chemistry classes—2.61/2.21. (Seymour et al. used nonweighted (NW) and weighted (W) means because they were comparing groups of widely different sizes. Therefore, I provide both chemistry class numbers in the order NW/W to give a more complete picture of their data.) In both 1998 and 1999, my classes' responses averaged 3.31. I stressed the importance of oral presentations, allowing students to work in groups to present and requiring them to submit their answers as groups, not individually. Seymour's chemistry group felt that students were nervous about presenting group results, possibly because students were embarrassed to give wrong answers orally (Weise et al. 1999).

Responses to questions 4 ("understanding the main concepts" and "understanding the relationship between concepts") were higher than average on the modular chemistry SALG forms—3.49/3.33 and 3.41/3.20. Results from my students' survey were 3.12 and 3.14, respectively, in 1998 and 3.51 and 3.49, respectively, in 1999 (table 3). Weise et al. (1999) felt that even with most sections giving very positive responses that students in modular classes underestimated their understanding. Students may have viewed chemistry as exceptionally rigorous and expected more difficulty than they encountered in the modular classes. On the other hand, many students see biology as less demanding because they think they can ease through by memorizing enough to do well on examinations. When I asked my students to learn the concepts so that they could explain them to others, many students probably reconsidered their earlier views on biology.

Advantages of the SALG Instrument

I do not have sufficient space here to discuss the value or difficulties with traditional course evaluations (of the instructor) but Weise et al. (1999) and Seymour et al. (2000) explain how the SALG instrument can answer questions that course evaluations cannot. They report that faculty comments often focus on how course evaluations do not provide useful feedback to improve teaching and that students' responses on course evaluations do not accurately reflect the effectiveness of their instructor's teaching. When used as the principal measure for tenure or promotion decisions, negative course evaluations can stifle needed faculty innovation in the classroom.

To improve college science teaching, instructors need to have suitable instruments to gauge student learning. In addition, instructors should be able to identify the most and least helpful parts of a course so that they can eliminate or change them before the next class offering. Evaluation committees need to judge teaching effectiveness, but some student evaluation responses discourage the introduction of unfamiliar, modern pedagogies.

The SALG instrument has the advantage of providing information about each aspect of the course as well as the course as a whole, concentrating on learning gains over personalities. Another of its advantages is that SALG is a tested instrument, available online, that is used by many comparable classes. The SALG instrument has allowed me to identify specifically what helps my students to learn and to compare my results to other introductory science class responses. The results from my students' feedback indicate that changing parts of the class was helpful to their learning, which benefits both me and the students.

References

Caprio, M.W., W.J. McIntosh, L.B. Micikas, and B. Shmaefsky. 1998. A model science literacy course. *Society for College Science Teachers Program and Abstracts* 18:16-17.

Heady, J.E. 1997. Journey toward better teaching in introductory biology. *College Teaching* 45(4): 123-127.

Heady, J.E. 2000. Assessment—A new way of thinking about learning—Now and in the future. *Journal of College Science Teaching* 29(6):415-421.

Kyle, W.C. 1997. The imperative to improve undergraduate education in science, mathematics, engineering, and technology. *Journal of Research in Science Teaching* 34(6): 547-549.

Lord, T.R. 1999. Are we cultivating 'couch potatoes' in our college science lectures? *Journal of College Science Teaching* 28(l): 59-62.

Schmidt, W.H., and C.C. McKnight. 1998. What can we really learn from TIMSS? *Science* 282:1830-1831.

Seymour, E., D.J. Wiese, A.-B. Hunter, and S.M. Daffinrud. 2000. Creating a better mousetrap: On-line student assessment of their learning gains. Paper presented to the National Meetings of the American Chemical Society Symposium, Using RealWorld Questions to Promote Active Learning, San Francisco, March 27.

Switzer, P.V., and J.I. Yoder. 1996. The academic treasure hunt: Checklist gives students motivation and control. *College Teaching* 44(3): 113-114.

Wiese, D., E. Seymour, and A.-B. Hunter. 1999. Report on a panel testing of the student assessment of their learning gains instrument by faculty using modular methods to teach undergraduate chemistry. Report to the Exxon Education Foundation. Bureau of Sociological Research, University of Colorado, Boulder.